T0328193

Cambridge Elements ☰

Elements in Decision Theory and Philosophy
edited by
Martin Peterson
Texas A&M University

COMMITMENT AND RESOLUTENESS IN RATIONAL CHOICE

Chrisoula Andreou
University of Utah

CAMBRIDGE
UNIVERSITY PRESS

University Printing House, Cambridge CB2 8BS, United Kingdom

One Liberty Plaza, 20th Floor, New York, NY 10006, USA

477 Williamstown Road, Port Melbourne, VIC 3207, Australia

314–321, 3rd Floor, Plot 3, Splendor Forum, Jasola District Centre, New Delhi – 110025, India

103 Penang Road, #05–06/07, Visioncrest Commercial, Singapore 238467

Cambridge University Press is part of the University of Cambridge.

It furthers the University's mission by disseminating knowledge in the pursuit of education, learning, and research at the highest international levels of excellence.

www.cambridge.org
Information on this title: www.cambridge.org/9781009211574
DOI: 10.1017/9781009211536

First published 2022

A catalogue record for this publication is available from the British Library.

ISBN 978-1-009-21157-4 Paperback
ISSN 2517-4827 (online)
ISSN 2517-4819 (print)

Commitment and Resoluteness in Rational Choice

Elements in Decision Theory and Philosophy

DOI: 10.1017/9781009211536
First published online: February 2022

Chrisoula Andreou
University of Utah

Author for correspondence: Chrisoula Andreou, c.andreou@utah.edu

Abstract: Drawing and building on the existing literature, this Element explores the interesting and challenging philosophical terrain where issues regarding cooperation, commitment, and control intersect. Section 1 discusses interpersonal and intrapersonal Prisoner's Dilemma situations and the possibility of a set of unrestrained choices adding up in a way that is problematic relative to the concerns of the choosers involved. Section 2 focuses on the role of precommitment devices in rational choice. Section 3 considers the role of resoluteness in rational choice and action. And Section 4 delves into some related complications concerning the nature of actions and the nature of intentions.

Keywords: commitment, cooperation, rational choice, resoluteness, self-control

ISBNs: 9781009211574 (PB), 9781009211536 (OC)
ISSNs: 2517-4827 (online), 2517-4819 (print)

Contents

Introduction: Why Commit?

Commitment is quite commonplace and, seemingly, quite significant, since it treats certain options as "off the table." My commitment to teaching my class this morning requires me to close off or put aside the possibility of doing some weight training instead. And my commitment to certain healthy eating practices requires me to close off or put aside the possibility of bringing a box of Twinkies as my lunch. Still, it might seem like commitment is either redundant or irrational – redundant if the option committed to is (taking into account its consequences) preferred over the alternatives, and irrational if the option committed to is dispreferred. But, as will become apparent, there are scenarios in which the ability to commit to a dispreferred alternative is necessary to reap the benefits of cooperation or self-control. This Element focuses on the interaction between cooperation, commitment, and control. Drawing from and building on the existing literature, including my own prior work in this space, I guide the reader through the interesting, challenging, and evolving philosophical terrain where issues regarding cooperation, commitment, and control intersect, adding some new contributions along the way.

As part of illustrating how choices restrained by commitments can sometimes pave the way to better outcomes, Section 1 discusses interpersonal and intrapersonal Prisoner's Dilemma situations and the possibility of a set of unrestrained choices adding up in a way that is problematic relative to the concerns of the choosers involved. The classic Prisoner's Dilemma situation involves two purely self-interested agents who, paradoxically, both do worse when they each follow their own self-interest than they would if they had restrained themselves and cooperated with one another.[1] In light of some key moves and refinements in debates regarding Prisoner's Dilemma situations, which I briefly review, paradigmatic examples of Prisoner's Dilemmas (PDs) now include interpersonal and intrapersonal cases in which the choosers need not be purely self-interested but do have a conflict of ends. In intrapersonal PDs, the choosers are generally assumed to be time slices of a person that (to some extent) discount the utility of future time slices. Like many interpersonal PDs, intrapersonal PDs often take the form of a free-rider problem, in which a good is not realized because each chooser refrains from contributing to its achievement, recognizing their individual contribution as trivial with respect to the realization of the good. Free-rider problems are normally associated with choosers who are partial to

---

[1] According to Martin Peterson (2015, 1), who corresponded with John F. Nash about the matter, the label "Prisoner's Dilemma" was coined by Albert W. Tucker during a lecture discussing Nash's work. (Tucker was Nash's thesis advisor.) A variation on the sort of example associated with the label is provided in Section 1.

themselves. But, building on debates regarding free-rider problems, I introduce the relatively neglected possibility of what I call "impartially benevolent free riders," understood as free riders motivated by impartial benevolence, and discuss the connection between such free riders and poor self-control. I conclude by emphasizing that, without restraint, certain benefits of cooperation and self-control may be out of reach.

Section 2 focuses on the role of precommitment devices in rational choice. As emphasized in the extensive literature on precommitment devices, such devices can helpfully alter choice situations or incentive structures in a way that makes it impossible or extremely costly to defect from a course of action (or a set of actions) that promises benefits of cooperation or self-control. Given the possibility of precommitting to a course of action, it might seem like Prisoner's Dilemma situations can be straightforwardly solved with precommitment devices once they are recognized and so should not persist. Relatedly, it might seem like an individual or collective that does not use a precommitment device to solve a so-called self-control problem is revealing a gap between proclaimed priorities and actual priorities and so should actually be diagnosed as hypocritical. But, as I've emphasized in my work on procrastination, this abstracts from the fact that suitable precommitment devices might not be easily identifiable or readily available.[2] Careful consideration of the case of the persistent procrastinator reveals how challenges associated with employing precommitment devices can prompt second-order procrastination, even for someone who is genuinely and seriously concerned about her failure to make progress on a proclaimed priority. Section 2 ends with some discussion of a particularly controversial precommitment device that is most commonly considered in discussions of mental illness but is of interest in a variety of cases of temptation. The device in question is a "Ulysses contract" and, as I explain, it seems particularly appropriate in intrapersonal free-rider cases of the sort considered in Section 1.

Section 3 considers the role of resoluteness in rational choice. Resoluteness involves a willingness to stick to a plan even if one believes that what the plan calls for conflicts with the preferences associated with one's current perspective. I survey and critically examine a variety of arguments aimed at supporting the view that resoluteness is a genuine possibility for a rational agent, including arguments that focus on the rationality of non-reconsideration, as well as arguments that first contrast evaluating actions directly and evaluating deliberative procedures and then focus on the rationality of acting in accordance with a beneficial deliberative procedure that allows for counter-preferential choice. Relatedly, I advance some new ideas and reasoning concerning resoluteness and

---

[2] See, for example, Andreou (2007a).

(what I call) "quasi-resoluteness" via an appeal to the importance of "meta-considerations" and an examination of cases of temptation in which there is a risk of the sort of impartially benevolent free riding introduced in Section 1. The arguments in this section of the Element suggest that incurring costs to precommit to an option by penalizing or eliminating alternatives may be a needlessly roundabout route to solving dilemmas in which certain benefits of cooperation or self-control cannot be realized without restraint. For, given the possibility of rational resoluteness, rational agents can reliably resolve to adhere to a cooperative or self-controlled course and follow through; precommitment devices might then only be needed to compensate for irrational irresoluteness.

Section 4 delves into some relevant complications concerning the nature of actions and the nature of intentions (condensing and synthesizing two strands of my prior work).[3] The complications are tied to the fact that correctly evaluating what an agent is doing at a particular point in time requires recognizing what the agent is doing at that point in time, and this is not a trivial matter, since what an agent is doing *at* a particular point in time is normally not contained *in* that point in time. As such, evaluating what an agent is doing at a particular point in time requires recognizing what dispositions, dynamics, and defaults are in play. After explaining the relevant complications, I explain how they impact some of the previous discussions in this Element. For example, I revisit my earlier discussion of impartially benevolent free riding and suggest that, despite initial appearances to the contrary in the sorts of cases of failure involving free riding motivated by impartial benevolence that I consider, *not* all of the doings (or omissions) occurring at points on the way to failure in relation to the goal at stake are at most trivially detrimental relative to the goal. I also revisit the apparent contrast between evaluating actions directly and evaluating deliberative procedures. I suggest that the contrast may be oversimplified, since one cannot be acting intentionally without integrating certain constraints into one's deliberative framework. I then highlight an alternative contrast, namely the contrast between "on-the-whole" evaluations and evaluations "through time," and suggest that so long as actions and deliberative procedures are evaluated in the same way, either both as wholes or, alternatively, both through time, one will not get conflicting verdicts regarding the best alternative.

Notably, throughout this Element, the notion of "preferences" in play is of preferences as "subjective comparative evaluations" (Hansson & Grüne-Yanoff 2017). Such evaluations can be, but are not necessarily, revealed in choice, since the latter might, in some cases, be explained instead by, for example, habit, an autopilot response, or non-deliberative follow-through on a prior plan.

---

[3] See, in particular, Andreou (2014a, 2016).

1 Interpersonal and Intrapersonal Prisoner's Dilemma Situations

1.1 Introduction

Prisoner's Dilemma situations illustrate the possibility of a set of unrestrained choices adding up in a way that is problematic relative to the concerns of the choosers involved. Complementing the extensive literature on interpersonal Prisoner's Dilemmas is a growing literature on intrapersonal Prisoner's Dilemmas. After briefly reviewing some key moves and refinements in debates regarding Prisoner's Dilemma situations, which include debates regarding free-rider problems, I introduce the relatively neglected possibility of what I call "impartially benevolent free riders" and discuss the connection between such free riders and cyclic preferences and poor self-control. I conclude by empha-sizing that, without restraint, certain benefits of cooperation and self-control may be out of reach.

1.2 The Classic Prisoner's Dilemma Situation

Two criminals have robbed a bank. There is enough evidence to convict each of them of the crime of illegally possessing a firearm, but more evidence is needed to convict either of them of the more serious crime of armed robbery. Although they are partners in crime, the criminals are purely self-interested, and each is looking to get off with as light a sentence as possible. Conviction of illegal possession of a firearm will result in a two-year prison sentence. Conviction of armed robbery will result in an additional ten-year prison sentence (for a total sentence of twelve years). There is a way for each criminal to provide decisive evidence against the other without incriminating himself. Recognizing this, the district attorney offers each criminal the following deal: provide decisive evidence against the other and your sen-tence will be reduced by a year. Each criminal considers the situation and recognizes that, whatever the other does, his best strategy is to provide the incriminating evidence requested. For if his partner provides incriminating evidence, he does better by providing incriminating evidence too, since doing so allows him to reduce the sentence he will face from twelve years to eleven. And if his partner does not provide incriminating evidence, he still does better by providing incriminating evidence, since doing so allows him to reduce the sentence he will face from two years to one. Since both criminals are purely self-interested, they each provide the district attorney with incriminating evidence and each ends up with an eleven-year sentence. Of course, had they both refused to provide any incriminating evidence, they would have each ended up with a two-year sentence. The district attorney's offer has thus landed them in a dilemma: self-interest prompts each of them to incriminate the other, but in both following their self-interest, they both end up worse off than they would have ended up if they had both restrained themselves.[4]

1.3 Prisoner's Dilemmas among Selfless Individuals

This Prisoner's Dilemma captures the essential feature of choice situations that now go by the name of Prisoner's Dilemmas. Roughly put, in a Prisoner's Dilemma, choices prompted by each chooser's concerns add up to an outcome that is worse, from the perspective of each chooser, than another that was available.[5] No prisoners need be involved; more than two choosers can be involved; and, interestingly, the choosers need not be purely self-interested. Indeed, a Prisoner's Dilemma situation might obtain even among totally selfless individuals if their selfless ends do not coincide. Consider, for example, Peter Vanderschraaf's shipwreck case, in which all that remains from the provisions that were brought along is one biscuit:

> If the survivors of a shipwreck are all perfectly selfless angels, then each will be tempted to leave all of what little food they have for the others. But if each angel yields to temptation completely, all will starve, even though each angel is acting so as to prevent the others from starving. Knowing this, the angels need to divide the food so that all get shares, even though this requires each of them to yield somewhat to the wishes of the others. (2006, 330)

Assuming that each selfless angel favors leaving the whole biscuit for others over eating some of it (knowing that all she can control is how much she leaves for them, not whether they will eat it), but also prefers that everyone eats some of the biscuit than that none eat any of it, this case involves a dilemma of the same structure as that in the original PD case presented: If each chooser proceeds selflessly (by, in this case, refusing to eat any of the biscuit), all do worse relative to their aim (of benefiting the others) than if they all show restraint relative to their aim (and all eat a bit themselves). That each agent's end is selfless does not interfere with the possibility of a PD being generated.

---

[4] As indicated in footnote 1, this is a variation on the sort of example associated with the label "Prisoner's Dilemma."

[5] More precisely, in a Prisoner's Dilemma, (1) each chooser has a dominant strategy in the sense that there is a single choice that invariably serves as her best possible choice, given her concerns, no matter how the others involved choose, and yet, (2) if each chooser follows her dominant strategy, the result is an outcome that is dominated in the sense that there is another possible outcome that all the choosers involved would have preferred. Notably, since each chooser in a PD has a dominant strategy, knowing how the other(s) will choose does not provide her with relevant information regarding her best choice.

1.4 Prisoner's Dilemmas, Cooperation, and the Circumstances of Justice

The preceding example figures in discussions regarding the connection between cooperation and justice. The circumstances of justice are prominently construed as the conditions under which a willingness to cooperate, where this involves a willingness to show restraint, or be restrained, for the sake of mutual benefit, is rationally called for. Thomas Hobbes famously cast justice as the rational solution to the chaos and destruction that purely self-interested agents – who treat others as a mere means to their own "conservation" and "delectation" – collectively generate in the absence of enforced ground rules (1668/1994, 75). David Hume (1951/1998, section 3, part 1) affirmed a connection between self-interest and justice when he argued that "extensive benevolence" would make justice redundant, since, insofar as one cares for others, one will take their interests into account even if there are no demands of justice compelling one to do so. But, for Hume, our need for justice is tied to our *limited* self-interest, which does not involve a complete indifference toward others but does involve "more concern for [our] own interest than for that of [our] fellows." Later theorists, including, perhaps most influentially, John Rawls, loosened the connection between self-interest and the circumstances of justice even further and sided with the now prevailing view that the circumstances of justice can obtain even among individuals who are not self-interested if they have different "plans of life" and "conceptions of the good" (Rawls 1971, 127) or, indeed, any conflict of ends, even if the ends they are committed to are not at all selfish. Relatedly, paradigmatic examples of PDs now include cases in which the choosers are not purely self-interested but have a conflict of ends.

1.5 Intrapersonal Prisoner's Dilemmas and Discounting

The recognition that PDs can be generated even among choosers who are strongly connected to one another by ties of care and concern facilitates the recognition of the possibility of *intra*personal PDs. Unlike in interpersonal PDs, in intrapersonal PDs, the choosers at issue are not separate individuals but the same individual at different times. Such PDs are easily generated when someone cares about her future (self) but also discounts future benefits, especially distant future benefits, assigning more weight to benefits that are imminent and so loom large.

It is generally recognized that human beings discount future utility, often favoring smaller, sooner rewards over larger, delayed rewards (e.g., $10 of treat-money today over $11 of treat-money tomorrow). Agents who discount future utility are fragmented into (what are sometimes referred to as) time-slice selves. Each time-slice self is not indifferent to the fate of the other time-slice selves, but closer time-slice selves are favored over more distant time-slice selves. Intrapersonal PDs exist when each time-slice self favors the achievement of a long-term goal but also prefers that the restraint needed to achieve the long-term goal be exercised not by her current self but by her future selves.

Suppose, for example, that I want my far-future self to experience a comfortable retirement and that this will require me to frequently save small amounts while I am still young. I have a little money that I can save today and put toward my retirement funds, but I consider the possibility of all (or most of) my future selves (with extra money) saving a little and realizing my long-term goal without any contribution from my current self, and I prefer that instead. Moreover, if I expect that none or few of my future selves (with extra money) are going to save, my long-term goal will not be met regardless of whether my current self contributes, and so my current self still favors contributing nothing. Still, all my time-slice selves prefer that we all save a little toward a comfortable retirement than that none do. I thus face an intrapersonal Prisoner's Dilemma situation.

It might be objected that if I really do discount future utility, favoring more proximate future time-slice selves over more distant future time-slice selves, I will not want the former time-slice selves to make any sacrifices for the latter time-slice selves, and so it will not be true that all of my time-slice selves prefer that they all show restraint than that none do. Notice, however, that discounting future utility need not involve invariably favoring rewards for earlier time-slice selves (no matter how minor) over rewards for later time-slice selves (no matter how crucial); depending on how exactly, and how much, future rewards are discounted, there is room for discounters to favor the sacrifice of small luxuries by more proximate future selves to ensure funds for necessities for more distant future selves.

But, if one discounts future utility at a rate that prompts one to currently favor spending a small amount of discretionary money today over saving it for twenty years from now, won't one also currently favor spending a small amount of discretionary money when one gets one's next paycheck (in the not-too-far future) over saving it for twenty years from then? The crucial thing to notice here is that while the answer would be "yes" given a fixed discount rate of, say, n percent per day, one's discount curve need not reflect a steady discount rate. And if (as evidence suggests is the norm) one's discount curve does not reflect a steady discount rate, it can be such that, while one currently favors spending a small amount of discretionary money today over saving it for twenty years from now, one also currently favors showing restraint when one gets one's next paycheck and saving a small amount of discretionary money then for twenty years from then.[6]

1.6 Interpersonal and Intrapersonal Free Riding Motivated by Partiality

The preceding intrapersonal Prisoner's Dilemma situation takes the form of a free-rider problem. In classic interpersonal free-rider problems, an agent who is partial to himself seeks to obtain a certain benefit without contributing to the realization of the benefit himself. Suppose, for example, that one wants to enjoy fairly clean air and that this requires a major reduction in the amount of polluting emissions in one's area. There is a major campaign encouraging individuals to take the bus to work rather than drive. One hopes the campaign will result in a significant improvement in air quality but, recognizing that whether this will occur does not hang on whether one participates because one's own participation would have no more than a trivial impact, one opts to proceed as usual and, hopefully, free ride off the efforts of others. The problem is that, insofar as others are similarly motivated, the result is "a tragedy of the commons." In a tragedy of the commons, a valued communal resource, such as clean air, is lost because, even though everyone would rather that all show restraint, with the result that the resource is preserved, than that none show restraint, with the result that the resource is lost, each acts on the recognition that, whatever others do, she is better off not showing restraint.[7]

In the retirement case, each time-slice self, though not indifferent to her future selves, is, nonetheless, somewhat partial to her current self and so favors shifting the burden of achieving the valued outcome of a comfortable retirement onto her future selves. In this case, tragedy results when the burden is not taken on by any of the time-slice selves, and the far-future selves that none of the time slices wanted to see suffer are miserably destitute.

1.7 The Impartially Benevolent Free Rider

Perhaps the most interesting under-explored aspect of free-rider situations is that they seem to make room for Prisoner's Dilemma situations in which the agents involved are all impartially benevolent.[8] (Of course, this possibility is precluded if it is *stipulated* that PDs must involve choosers who do not

---

[6] See Ainslie (2001, chapter 3).

[7] The label "tragedy of the commons" can be traced to Hardin (1968). For an influential general discussion of the logic of collective action, see Olson (1965).

[8] See Andreou (2010, 207) for some remarks that verge on recognizing this possibility. This aspect of free-rider situations is related to the puzzling "moral mathematics" in cases like Derek Parfit's

fully share ends; but this stipulation can appropriately be put aside if the dilemma in PDs – which is, roughly put, that choices prompted by each chooser's concerns add up to an outcome that is worse, from the perspective of each chooser, than another that was available – is possible even for choosers who do fully share ends.) Consider the following case. J wants to lose enough weight so that he looks about as trim as he was when he got married (and fit into size 32 pants). It is easy to see how J might find himself in a dilemma if he discounts future utility. But suppose he does not discount future utility; suppose, in particular, that his time slices are not at all partial to themselves but are impartially benevolent. A dilemma can still arise. For, as long as it is true that whether the desired outcome will occur does not hang on whether this particular time slice, say J_n, sacrifices his enjoyment by, for instance, passing up a brownie bite (since J_n's sacrifice will have no more than a trivial impact), J_n, as well as his past and future time slices, can, motivated by impartial benevolence, reason as follows: J_n's sacrifice will have no more than a trivial impact on J's appearance; so, whatever his future time slices do, it is preferable that J_n enjoy the brownie bite and put off dieting for now. Even an impartially benevolent agent can favor allowing for some free rides when the cost to the whole is trivial enough. The problem, of course, is that there is nothing distinctive about J_n, and so the sort of benevolent thinking under consideration can, like free riding motivated by partiality, result in an important goal never being met.

The same sort of challenge can cause trouble for a unified collective. Consider, for instance,

> a collective that values a healthy community, values luxuries whose production or use promotes a carcinogenic environment, and believes that if it does not curb its consumption, the health of the community will be seriously damaged. This collective might rightly think that if it is going to curb consumption, it is better off starting next month rather than right away. For the community can then enjoy another month of luxury living and this will not take the community's members from a state of decent health to a state of poor health. Yet, if the collective opts for a high level of consumption month after month, the health of the community will be seriously damaged. (Andreou 2006a, 104)

1.8 Unification, Fragmentation, and Cyclic Preferences

Though they can be divided into component time slices or selves, both the temporally extended individual J and the collective just described are *unified*

"Drops of Water" case (1984, 76), at least if contributing one's pint of water has some cost (of, e.g., effort or opportunity). See, relatedly, Glover (1975), Kagan (2011), and Temkin (2012).

in the sense that, by hypothesis, there is no conflict of ends *between* different choosing slices or selves; all the choosing slices or selves (including every time slice, J_x, of J in J's case and, alternatively, every time slice of the collective in the community case) have the same shared interests. Each choosing slice or self is, however, *fragmented* in the sense that it itself has potentially conflicting interests that it must consider when it is making choices. For example, J_n must consider both his interest in J's appearance and his interest in J's culinary delight – interests that he shares with all of J's time slices. Such fragmentation can raise the same sorts of challenges to effective decision-making as is faced by agents with conflicting ends. Notice, in particular, that such fragmentation can generate not only a Prisoner's Dilemma situation but also related *cyclic* preferences.

Preferences over a set of options qualify as cyclic if the options cannot be ordered from most preferred to least preferred (even allowing for ties) because the preference structure puts the options in a "loop" wherein, for example, O_1 is preferred to O_2, O_2 is preferred to O_3, . . ., O_{n-1} is preferred to O_n, but O_n is preferred to O_1. We know from Condorcet's paradox that if a group of agents who do not share preferences vote on options in accordance with their preferences, the resulting "social preference" can be cyclic, even if each agent's preferences are not.[9] For example, if A's ordering of O_1, O_2, and O_3 from most preferred to least preferred is O_3, O_2, O_1, B's ordering is O_2, O_1, O_3, and C's ordering is O_1, O_3, O_2, then the "social preference" that results from majority rule pair-wise voting on the options results in a preference loop in which O_3 is preferred to O_2, O_2 is preferred to O_1, but O_1 is preferred to O_3. Relatedly, an agent with stable preferences, but *multiple* interests, and a prioritization system that appeals to thresholds, can have cyclic preferences even if the agent's ranking of a set of options relative to a single dimension of concern is invariably acyclic (i.e., not cyclic). Suppose, for example, that O_n is the option of consuming n brownie bites this month, and that, in terms of their fit with culinary delight, A's ordering of options O_1, O_2, . . ., O_{300} from most preferred to least preferred is O_{300}, . . ., O_2, O_1; by contrast, in terms of their fit with dieting, A's ordering of options O_1, O_2, . . ., O_{300} from most preferred to least preferred is O_1, O_2, . . ., O_{300}. Suppose further that, taking into account both factors, A prefers an option that fits with dieting above an option that fits with culinary delight unless the difference between the options in terms of their contribution to weight loss is too small to make a significantly noticeable difference to anyone judging A's appearance. Then, as suggested by J's case,

---

Condorcet's paradox is named after the Marquis de Condorcet, who pinpointed the paradox as part of his pioneering work in social choice theory. See de Condorcet (1785).

A's preferences, taking into account his multiple interests, can be cyclic, with O_{n+1} preferred to O_n, for all n between 1 and 299, but O_1 preferred to O_{300}.[10]

1.9 Free Riding, Procrastination, and Poor Self-Control

As is suggested by J's case and by the case of the unified collective, there is an interesting connection between impartially benevolent free riding and procrastination.[11] In cases of impartially benevolent free riding, contribution to a desired outcome is locally waived because the impact of the waiver is individually trivial and the waiver allows for the gain of some benefit. In many cases, including J's and the case of the unified collective, the local waiver amounts to putting off contributing to the desired outcome in accordance with the preference to initiate contributory action at time period $n+1$ over initiating contributory action at time period n. The problem is that, if this process is iterated, the burden of contributory action is pushed off indefinitely and the result is that the desired outcome is not achieved. Such cases of procrastination can be modeled as cases in which the agent finds herself following cyclic preferences of the following form to an outcome she deems unacceptable (even though acceptable outcomes were available): initiating contributory action (or restraint) at time $n+1$ is preferred to initiating contributory action at time n, and yet initiating contributory action early on, say in time period 1, is preferred to initiating contributory action very late, say in time period 100.[12] Such cases of procrastination figure as familiar examples of self-imposed frustration and poor self-control, where the sort of poor self-control at issue involves not reduced control by the self, but the self fully controlling behavior in a way that is poorly suited for success.

---

[10] See Quinn (1993) for related discussion, including discussion of his structurally similar famous case of the "self-torturer." In Quinn's intriguing case, "a medical device ... enables doctors to apply electric current to the body in [tiny] increments," with no noticeable differences in comfort experienced "between adjacent settings" but notable or major differences in comfort experienced "between settings that are sufficiently far apart" (198). A participant, who has the device attached to him "in some conveniently portable form" (198), will get $10,000 each time he dials up the device one setting. Given that the participant's state from one setting to the next is not noticeably different (or at least not noticeably different enough for the participant to be able to confidently distinguish between "adjacent" states), he understandably prefers to advance a setting each time he has the opportunity to do so (given the large monetary reward); but he also prefers not having advanced at all over repeatedly advancing and ending up rich but in a state of excruciating pain. The participant's preferences are thus understandably cyclic. Moreover, the participant is, as Quinn emphasizes, "not alone in his predicament. Most of us are like him in one way or another. We like to eat but also care about our appearance. Just one more bite will give us pleasure and won't make us look fatter; but very many bites will" (199).

[11] For some remarks that do not appeal to impartially benevolent free riding but are nonetheless suggestive, see Andreou (2010, 207).

[12] See Andreou (2007b).

1.10 Cyclic Preferences and Money Pumps

At this point, it might be suggested that the plight of the procrastinator should, like the famous "money-pump argument," be interpreted as supporting the conclusion that cyclic preferences are rationally impermissible. According to the money-pump argument, an agent who follows her cyclic preferences can be pumped for money since, assuming she is willing to pay a tiny fee to trade a less preferred option for a more preferred option, she can be led, via a series of trades each of which costs her a little, back to an option she already had.[13] Suppose, for example, that K prefers O_1 over O_2, and O_2 over O_3, but O_3 over O_1. Suppose also that K has O_1 and a bit of spending money. If she has the opportunity to trade O_1 and a penny for O_2, her preferences will prompt her to do so. Similarly, given the chance, her preferences will prompt her to trade O_2 and a penny for O_3. If she then has the opportunity to trade O_3 and a penny for O_1, her preferences will prompt her to trade yet again. This lands her with the option she started off with but with three less pennies. And this round of trade offers can easily be followed by another. K is thus susceptible to being money pumped, which makes her preferences seem problematic. But perhaps the correct conclusion to draw is that an agent with cyclic preferences should not naively follow her preferences; instead, she should proceed in a way that is responsive to the dilemma that can be generated by them in certain contexts. (More on this later.) This position warns against the potential pitfalls associated with cyclic preferences while allowing that the preferences themselves might be sensibly generated by "rationally innocent" concerns (such as, for example, J's concern with altering his appearance and his concern with culinary delight).[14]

1.11 Conclusion

Interpersonal and intrapersonal Prisoner's Dilemma situations, including situations involving free riders motivated by partiality and situations involving impartially benevolent free riders, show that choosers can be better off all showing restraint or being restrained than all acting without restraint. Without restraint, certain benefits of cooperation and self-control may be out of reach. I thus turn, in the next two sections of this Element, to two forms of restraint and to debates regarding their role in rational choice.

---

[13] The original presentation of "the money-pump argument" can be found in Davidson, McKinsey, & Suppes (1955).

[14] The quoted phrase is borrowed from Tenenbaum & Raffman (2012).

2 Precommitting

2.1 Introduction

In this section of the Element, I focus on the use of precommitment devices in rational choice. Precommitment devices can helpfully alter choice situations or incentive structures in a way that makes it impossible or extremely costly to defect from a course of action (or a set of actions) that promises benefits of cooperation or self-control. Given the possibility of precommitting to a course of action, it might be suggested that Prisoner's Dilemma situations should be transitory since they can be straightforwardly solved with precommitment devices once they are recognized. Relatedly, it might be suggested that an individual or collective that does not use a precommitment device to solve a so-called self-control problem is revealing a gap between proclaimed priorities and actual priorities and so should actually be diagnosed as hypocritical. But this abstracts from the fact that suitable precommitment devices might not be easily identifiable or readily available. As suggested by the case of the persistent procrastinator (which I will get to shortly), challenges associated with employing precommitment devices can prompt second-order procrastination, even for someone who is genuinely and seriously concerned about her failure to make progress on a proclaimed priority.[15] Toward the end of this section, I turn to a controversial precommitment device that is most commonly considered in discussions of mental illness but is of interest in a variety of cases of temptation. The device in question is a Ulysses contract, and, as I explain, it seems particularly appropriate in intrapersonal free-rider cases of the sort considered in Section 1.

2.2 Mutual Coercion Mutually Agreed Upon

Recall the classic interpersonal Prisoner's Dilemma situation involving two caught criminals and consider the following question: What could two criminals who anticipate the possibility of finding themselves in a Prisoner's Dilemma situation do to avert this threat? As suggested in plenty of mobster movies, they can employ the Hobbesian strategy of incurring a cost to embed themselves in a system in which they will be severely penalized if they provide incriminating evidence against their partner. Although, in this case, the system would presumably be an underground (i.e., illegal) system, the strategy is Hobbesian in that it involves setting up a "common power to fear" that changes the incentive structure so that betraying one's partner is foolish. This is a form of "mutual coercion mutually agreed upon" and is the most familiar precommitment device

---

[15] See Andreou (2007a).

for solving interpersonal Prisoner's Dilemma situations.[16] For Hobbes, it is also the foundation of justice, which is supposed to involve restraint (which, in Hobbes's picture, amounts to restraining ground rules enforced by a coercive power) and advantage (which accounts for the rationality of generating the restraining ground rules).

Notably, so long as the system that is introduced changes the incentive structure so that one is better off being loyal to one's partner than betraying him, the mechanism involved can vary. In some cases, the dilemma might be more simply solved with rewards for loyalty rather than penalties for betrayal.

2.3 Self-Constraint and Self-Control

What about in intrapersonal cases? Return to J's case. How might J precommit to losing weight? One possibility is for one of his early selves to make a choice that constrains the choices of his later selves. Suppose, for example, that J lives on an isolated beet farm, and it is a hassle for J to get to the grocery store except on Saturday mornings when he gets a lift there and back from a friend. Then J can constrain a week's worth of his future selves to comply with his diet by spending their money – he is paying by credit – on healthy staples. Even if it is not impossible for him to go to the grocery store mid-week and buy a family-sized value pack of brownie bites (as was his custom on Saturdays until recently) or even just a single brownie bite, it may be inconvenient enough that, all things considered, he is not inclined to do so. Moreover, this system may allow J to lose weight even if J's shopping selves benevolently free ride on his dieting selves and each consumes a single brownie bite while shopping on Saturday mornings.

Is this a case of effective self-control via justified self-constraint? J does seem to be solving his self-control problem by constraining himself for his own good. But, given J's division into time-slice selves, this description may seem to involve equivocation. Doesn't the constraining self differ from the constrained selves, and, if so, aren't the labels self-control and self-constraint misleading because the control and constraint are still really by one self over another (or multiple others), with the constrained selves having had no say in the set up?

To sort through all this, it is worth contrasting J's case with a classic, bolder case of so-called self-constraint. The case I have in mind is the much-discussed case of Ulysses and the Sirens, which figures in Homer's *Odyssey*.[17] While on his journey home after the Trojan War, Ulysses is warned about being drawn into peril by the enchanting singing of the Sirens. To ensure that he and his crew

---

[16] See Hardin (1968), from which the quoted phrase is borrowed.

[17] For some influential philosophical discussion of the case, see, for example, Elster (1984, 2000).

are not tempted to veer off course, Ulysses orders his companions to tie him to the mast of the ship and then plugs up their ears with beeswax so that they are not swayed by the singing and he cannot interfere with their progress. As anticipated, once Ulysses hears the singing of the Sirens, he is, at least temporarily, deeply impacted by the experience, and desperately signals that he wants to be unbound. But his initial plan is successful and they promptly sail off.

According to the interpretation of the case that I want to focus on, Ulysses' preferences are transformed by the Siren's singing, and his earlier guiding aim of getting home is replaced by the altogether different guiding aim of remaining among the Sirens. In this case, the disconnect between Ulysses' earlier constraining self and his later constrained self seems radical enough to suggest that there is not enough unity between them to support thinking of the case as deeply different from cases in which one self is controlling another.

J's case is different. By hypothesis, J's losing weight is a goal that all of J's time slices endorse. They also all see the desirability of allowing for some free rides and the threat of such free rides becoming the rule rather than the exception. As such, they can, univocally, endorse a system that includes constraints meant to avert this threat.[18] Moreover, insofar as they are not even partial to themselves and so share a single perspective, there is enough unity between them to interpret them as collectively constituting a single persisting agent, namely J's temporally extended self. Given this interpretation, something done or endured by a time slice of J is also plausibly understood as done or endured by J. And so there is room for J's precommitment strategy to count as self-control via self-constraint.

2.4 Procrastination, Hypocrisy, and Second-Order Procrastination

Given the possibility of self-control via self-constraint, it might be suggested that a self-proclaimed procrastinator is really just a hypocrite because, upon recognizing that one has a procrastination problem, one can promptly solve it by employing a precommitment device; insofar as one does not employ a precommitment device, one reveals that one does not genuinely favor acting sooner rather than later. But this oversimplifies matters. For it may not be a simple matter to settle on a suitable precommitment device; moreover, in some cases, the only available precommitment devices might be too disadvantageous to be rationally employable.

When there are obstacles to settling on a suitable precommitment device, an agent might be susceptible to second-order procrastination.[19] Consider the

---

[18] See, relatedly, my discussion in subsection 2.7.

[19] See Andreou (2007a), which includes discussion of a variation of the following example and of the examples in subsection 2.5.

following variation on an example familiar from the economic literature on procrastination: An employee keeps putting off deciding how to invest her retirement funds because arriving at a good investment strategy poses a difficult deliberative task. In the meantime, she leaves all her retirement funds in the money market account that they are automatically funneled into by her employer, recognizing that this is not a good place for the funds and set on moving the funds as soon as she settles on a better option. Here the agent's first order procrastination problem persists even though it is recognized because the solution is not obvious. What's ironic here is that the agent's commitment to make a good decision fuels her second-order procrastination, which, if it persists, leaves her with what she recognizes as among the worst long-term investment strategies. Notably, higher-order procrastination need not be limited to second-order procrastination. As will be suggested in the next subsection, attempts at dealing with second-order procrastination need to be sensitive to the possibility of even higher-order procrastination.

A variation on J's case provides us with a different but also extremely challenging scenario – one in which the only available precommitment device that can help the agent achieve his end is too disadvantageous to be rationally employable. Suppose that, unlike in the case in which J lives on an isolated beet farm, J is located in a big city in which affordable tasty treats are readily available at every turn. Suppose further that J has tried every weight-loss tactic that he has heard of and is now considering the only remaining available precommitment device, namely surgically reducing the size of his stomach so that his future selves literally cannot consume too many calories (at least for a while). J's doctor advises against the procedure since it poses great health risks (unlike the bit of extra weight J has put on). Although J is not dieting for his health but his appearance, he does not want to incur any great health risks. He thus decides against the procedure and remains in his dilemma. Although J's failure to solve his problem is not a case of second-order procrastination, since J promptly and plausibly concludes that no good precommitment device is available, it is, as in cases of second-order procrastination, one in which the clear obstacles to the agent's solving his (first-order) procrastination problem speak against dismissing the agent as a hypocrite.

2.5 Second-Order Procrastination and Mandatory Implementation Plans

Like a single agent, a collective, even if it is fairly unified, can face obstacles to solving a recognized procrastination problem. Consider, to take a case I have explored in detail in my prior work, a collective that procrastinates with respect to environmental preservation despite assertions of serious concern.

> Since [the collective] cannot stop having an impact on the environment altogether, the bright line of complete abstention from interference is not something it can even aim at. Instead, [it] must face the daunting task of finding and assessing the feasibility and advantages and disadvantages of different ways of striking a balance between preservation and utilization. In addition, given how high the stakes are, [it is] likely to want to defer accepting a proposed solution that calls for significant sacrifices until the proposal has been subject to a great deal of critical scrutiny . . .. Furthermore, as politicians are presumably acutely aware, the collective resources needed to cover these costs can be applied with greater immediate effect to more manageable problems with more transparent solutions. It is thus tempting to put off [settling on] a solution to procrastination with respect to environmental preservation . . . for a while longer, and a while longer, and a while longer . . . (Andreou 2007a, 245–246)

An interesting potential solution in this case involves mandatory implementation plans.[20] As elaborated on in my detailed discussion of the case in Andreou (2007a), the federal clean air laws provide an illustration of this possibility (though there are complications that interfere with their effectiveness that I will not delve into here). In addition to setting fairly distant deadlines for achieving certain goals tied to protecting air quality, the laws require states to promptly develop implementation plans for achieving the long-term goals. If no implementation plan is adopted and adhered to, substantial penalties are applied right away, even if the deadline for achieving the goal is still in the distant future. These laws thus increase the current cost of second-order procrastination. And, importantly,

> because the laws sidestep the difficult task of providing implementation plans (leaving it for after the laws have changed our incentive structure), procrastination need not be an overwhelming problem with respect to the task of creating the laws. In short, the laws [have the potential to] discourage second-order procrastination without their creation being stymied by higher-order procrastination. (Andreou 2007a, 246–247)

2.6 Ulysses Contracts

The possibility of generating binding constraints to save oneself from a self-control problem raises interesting questions about the legitimacy of enforcing

---

[20] For interesting and influential discussion concerning the potential effectiveness of implementation plans or intentions in *intra*personal cases of temptation, see, for example, Gollwitzer & Schaal (1998). The connection between implementation intentions and automatic follow-through ties into discussions regarding resolutions and rational non-reconsideration, which will be broached in subsection 3.2.

so-called Ulysses contracts. The contracts are advance directives in which some suitable third party is instructed to force one to perform or abstain from some action regardless of one's anticipated change of heart and ensuing resistance. The contracts are named after Ulysses (of Homer's tale of Ulysses and the Sirens), who, as discussed above, instructed his companions to tie him to the mast of his ship so that he would not, upon hearing the enchanting singing of the Sirens, change his course in order to remain with them rather than head home as planned.

A variety of interesting philosophical contributions on Ulysses contracts can be found in work regarding mental illness.[21] The cases of interest are not those in which someone's mental illness has rendered him at least temporarily incompetent, but instead cases in which someone seems to be in the early stages of relapsing into a bad state but is not yet making decisions that support an assessment of incompetence. In cases involving incompetence, intervention is considered morally and legally permissible even without the existence of a Ulysses contract. It is in suspected early-stage relapse cases that a Ulysses contract is potentially useful and yet also highly controversial because, by hypothesis, were there no Ulysses contract, interference would not be warranted, and it's not clear that the earlier self's intention to intervene in order to benefit his later self should override the competent later self's preferences against the intervention.

Consider the case of someone with bipolar disorder who is averse to the side effects of his medications and often finds himself tempted to get off them for a while, particularly when things seem to be going pretty well.[22] Sometimes these temporary medication-hiatus experiments go okay, but often the result is a manic phase that precipitates soon-to-be regretted behavior. After multiple setbacks, the patient seeks to bind himself to treatment via a Ulysses contract. The hope is that the contract will ensure that if, at some point, the patient's loved ones realize that he is not taking his medication, he will be admitted for psychiatric care regardless of whether he protests, even if he is deemed mentally competent and definitely could not be admitted without his consent apart from the contract. Debate about whether such a Ulysses contract is legitimately enforceable is often focused on the question of whether enforcement promotes or, instead, interferes with the agent's autonomy. As will become apparent, it is, at this point, fruitful to turn to a discussion of temptation, focusing, in particular,

---

[21] See, for instance, Dresser (1982, 1984), Savulescu & Dickenson (1998), Quante (1999), and Spellecy (2003). For a more general influential philosophical discussion of self-binding contracts, ethics, and the law, see Schelling (1984).

[22] A variation on this case is presented in Andreou (2018a).

on cases of anticipated temptation, which, as suggested by Ulysses' case, can generate a wish or demand for enforceable Ulysses contracts.

2.7 Temptation

Cases of anticipated temptation often generate a fear of being led down a self-defeating course of action and a desire to block this possibility by signing on for interference that would otherwise be uncalled for. I focus, in this subsection, on cases that are particularly challenging in relation to justifying interference, namely cases in which the later self plausibly maintains that she has carefully considered the options and is simply seeking to act on her ranking of the options (and so in accordance with her better judgment). In my view, even in such cases, interference may be justifiable in a way that appeals to, rather than dismissing, the later self's preferences.[23]

Return to the two intrapersonal free-rider cases from Section 1. The first case, in which free riding is motivated by partiality, is the case in which I want my far-future self to experience a comfortable retirement but, due to partiality to my current self, prefer that this long-term goal be realized without any contribution from my current self. The second case, in which free riding is motivated by impartial benevolence, is the case in which J wants to lose weight to improve his appearance but, recognizing that a current sacrifice will have no more than a trivial impact on his appearance, prefers, out of impartial benevolence, that his current self get to enjoy a brownie bite. Importantly, in both cases, all of the agent's time slices prefer that they all contribute to the relevant cause than that none do, which is part of what makes the situations Prisoner's Dilemmas.

Now suppose these agents seek to employ Ulysses contracts to bind their future selves to contribute to the relevant cause by instructing, say, a loved one to "force the issue." Can enforcement be justified from the point of view of the preferences of each later self who would be constrained to act contrary to his preferences? Or does enforcement amount to illegitimately favoring the preferences of one self (the earlier self) at the expense of another (each later self)? The idea that enforcement is justifiable even from the point of view of the preferences of each later self might be grounded in the following reasoning: Because all the time slices (including each later constrained time slice) prefer that the long-term goal be realized, when there is a threat of failure due to systematic free riding, every time slice (including each later constrained time slice) has an interest in having dilemma-resolving Ulysses contracts accepted

---

[23] See Andreou (2008).

as legitimately enforceable, even if this means that they too will be forced to contribute to the long-term goal.[24]

Importantly, there are several purported cases of temptation in which the same sort of justification is not available. Indeed, depending on how it is embellished, Ulysses case might be one in which enforcement amounts simply to favoring the preferences of one self (the earlier self) at the expense of another (the later self). To see this, consider first the following related, more familiar case.[25] Suppose K will be going into labor soon and has decided not to get an epidural because she finds the prospect of drug-free childbirth inspiring. However, in the midst of childbirth, she has a change of heart and asks for an epidural. The experience of excruciating pain prompts her to rerank the options and favor a medicated childbirth experience. Suppose that her earlier self knew that her later self was in store for excruciating pain but still favored a drug-free childbirth and, anticipating resistance by her later self, prepared a Ulysses contract instructing that all proceed as planned despite any protestations by her later self. Her later self can plausibly complain that enforcement in such situations cannot be justified from her point of view; the experience of excruciating pain has led her to the view that the benefits of a drug-free birth are not worth the cost. She does not share a goal with her earlier self that gives her a stake in accepting the Ulysses contract as legitimately enforceable. Ulysses, when sailing past the Sirens while tied to the mast of the ship, might be in a similar situation. The experience of the incredibly sweet singing of the Sirens may have led him to view the benefits of quickly sailing past as not worth the costs of missing this amazing transformative experience, which is hard to deeply appreciate in the abstract. As such, he too may not share a goal with his earlier self that gives him a stake in accepting the Ulysses contract as legitimately enforceable.

The case of the individual with bipolar disorder described above may be such that the individual's later self shares a goal with his earlier self that makes enforcement justifiable from the point of view of his later self. If this self also has the goal of taking precautions so that he does not relapse into a bad state but prefers to exempt his current self from contributing to that goal, he may be in the sort of Prisoner's Dilemma situation that may give him a stake in having a dilemma-resolving Ulysses contract accepted as legitimately enforceable, even if this means that he too will be forced to contribute to the long-term goal.

---

[24] See Andreou (2008), though I there discuss the matter in somewhat different terms and, in particular, without mention of a "dilemma-resolving" device that can address "systematic free riding."

[25] The case is a variation on an example in Andreou (2014b), though in that case there is no Ulysses contract in play.

2.8 Conclusion

As we have seen, precommitment devices can helpfully alter choice situations or incentive structures in a way that makes it impossible or extremely costly to defect from a course that promises benefits of cooperation or self-control; however, sometimes, suitable precommitment devices can be hard to come by, and often there are costs associated with changing the choice situation or incentive structure that would not have to be incurred if agents could resolve to voluntarily show restraint. The next section of this Element focuses on the controversial role of resoluteness in rational choice.

3 Resoluteness

3.1 Introduction

The sort of precommitment discussed in Section 2 changes things so that deviating from the option committed to is either no longer within one's power or else is dispreferred all things considered. It is thus a form of commitment that does not require any resoluteness, where resoluteness involves a willingness to stick to a plan (given one's current situation) even if one believes that one can deviate and that what the plan calls for conflicts with one's current preferences or would conflict with one's current preferences if one were to disengage from one's previous decision and reconsider things from one's current perspective. Is resoluteness a genuine possibility for a rational agent? If so, incurring costs to precommit to an option by penalizing or eliminating alternatives might seem like a needlessly roundabout route to solving dilemmas in which certain benefits of cooperation or self-control cannot be realized without restraint. For, given the possibility of rational resoluteness, couldn't rational agents reliably resolve to adhere to a cooperative or self-controlled course and follow through? This section delves into debate regarding rationality and resoluteness.

3.2 Plans and Rational Non-Reconsideration

Agents sometimes plan on certain actions in advance and then follow through without further deliberation. This seems perfectly appropriate if there is inadequate time for deliberation when the time for action arrives, or if there is no reason to believe that one might, after deliberation, favor an option other than the one prescribed by one's plan. Moreover, if one invariably reconsidered one's plans upon reaching the time of action, advance planning would arguably be pointless.

Although these points suggest that there is room for rational non-reconsideration of prior plans, it might be wondered whether non-reconsideration could be rational in cases in which time for reconsideration is readily available and one expects that reconsideration would lead one to opt for a different alternative. Consider the case of Homer:

> Homer has not been getting much exercise, and it is starting to show. He judges, and desires, that he should do something more active. He resolves to go for a daily run, starting next Saturday morning. But as his alarm goes off early on Saturday, his thoughts start to change. He is feeling particularly comfortable in bed, and the previous week had been very draining. He could start his running next weekend. And does he really want to be an early-morning runner at all? (Holton 2009, 138)

At this point, mightn't Homer see where such thinking is going and rationally retreat from reopening the question of whether to go running this morning, insisting to himself that he stick with his resolution? This is a tricky question. If Homer is suspicious of the reasoning capacities of his current self, he might resist reconsidering on the grounds that he expects his revised conclusion to be based on reasoning clouded by the experience of temptation. But why should the experience of lying in his comfortable bed after a draining week be dismissed as clouding his judgment rather than informing it (by making him viscerally aware of how burdensome his proposed plan is). As Holton explains, "Homer's judgements are not crazy. The bed *is* very comfortable; he *has* had a hard week. Indeed it is far from obvious that someone in Homer's situation should go for a run every morning; physical fitness is surely not a prerequisite of the good life" (2009, 139). Holton concludes that

> [i]f it is rational for Homer to stick with his resolution, this is at least partly because he has formed it. Suppose he had decided, reasonably enough, that early-morning runs were not for him: that, all things considered, he would rather go on as before and live with the consequences. It is hard to think that such a decision would be irrational. But, relative to that decision, getting up early on Saturday morning to go for a run would look irrational. At the very least, there is no sense in which Homer would be rationally *required* to get up, in the way that he is after having made the resolution. (2009, 139)

But is Homer really rationally required to get up rather than to reconsider his resolution? If Homer has had a genuine change of heart about the value of getting in shape, it's hard to see why reconsideration is not in order.[26] What if

---

[26] This is so even if one accepts, with Broome (2001), that one is normatively required to act on intentions that one has not repudiated, since the requirement leaves room for Homer to repudiate his intention. (Notably, for Broome, "an unrepudiated intention constitutes a normative requirement rather than a reason" (2001, 114) and so even if Homer does not repudiate his intention, Broome is not committed to saying that Homer has bootstrapped a reason into existence. For some foundational discussion regarding bootstrapping, see Bratman (1987), especially chapter 2, section 2.5.)

Homer has not had a change of heart about the value of getting in shape but is just inclined to make an exception for his current self? Is Homer required to get up in that case? And if so, why? As is clear from the last quote from Holton, Homer's case of temptation is not to be interpreted as a case in which the ranking that favors not going for a run every Saturday morning can be dismissed as in-and-of-itself irrational; by hypothesis, it cannot, and this makes the case more philosophically challenging. Why would refusing to reconsider one's resolution be appropriate when the resolution conflicts with a sensible all-things-considered ranking that is quite clearly supported by one's current perspective?[27]

3.3 Resoluteness and the Agent's Standpoint

While defenders of resoluteness remain on the defensive, with skepticism about resoluteness figuring as standard in decision theory,[28] I turn, in this subsection to what I see as a particularly suggestive and in some ways promising recent philosophical defense of a version of resoluteness that is supposed to illuminate cases of temptation such as the case of Homer. The defense is provided by Michael Bratman in his work on temptation and the agent's standpoint. According to Bratman, "in engaging in planning agency we are committed to giving significance to how our planned activities will look to us as our plan progresses into the future" (2018, 160). This creates room for the following "intuitive idea": a planning agent's standpoint can be affected by anticipated regret. More specifically, in certain cases of temptation where the agent antici-pates that if she abandons her resolution or even just makes an exception for her current self, she will come to regret it, there will be pressure on the agent to shift her current evaluative judgment so that it is in line with her future evaluative judgment. In short, the planning agent's standpoint will not automatically be determined by her current evaluative judgment apart from any consideration of the possibility that her evaluative judgment will shift over time. The idea is that even if her current evaluative judgment is in-and-of-itself permissible, the agent's standpoint may not be adequately captured by that single judgment. Return to Homer's case. Even if Homer, in the moment of temptation, has had a genuine change of heart about the value of getting in shape, it may be that this shift in evaluative judgment is temporary. If it is, and if Homer is not too naive and myopic to "see the writing on the wall," he will, if he is a rational planning agent, not just dismiss his future regret as irrelevant. To the contrary, he will allow his anticipated regret to influence his current evaluative judgment,

---

[27] I provide a fairly detailed discussion of my worries regarding Holton's view in Andreou (2014b).
[28] See Steele & Stefánsson (2020) for a sense of the current state of play.

recognizing that, except insofar as his current self is appropriately influenced by the potentially shifting attitudes of the temporally extended self implicated in his plans, his standpoint is not just the standpoint of his current self. There may, therefore, be rational pressure on him to stick with his prior resolution.

Bratman's position ingeniously combines what might seem like two incompatible desiderata. First, it allows that there is room for a rational agent experiencing temptation to adhere to a prior plan even if she finds, upon evaluating her options, that she favors abandoning it. Second, it allows for "the rational priority of present evaluation," according to which "if, when the dust settles, the agent does indeed have a relevant judgment at [the time of action] concerning which alternative would be strictly best at [that time], then, if that agent is functioning rationally, she will opt for that alternative (if she opts for any alternative at all)" (Bratman 2018, 153). Bratman is, I think, correct in seeing his realization of this combination as a major virtue of his account. And, though I will now turn to a critique of his position, I will ultimately suggest a way of moving beyond Bratman's view that retains this virtue.

3.4 A Dilemma

Bratman's position faces a dilemma: On the one hand, insofar as an agent's evaluative judgments are changing over time, it cannot be safely assumed that there is a single standpoint that speaks for the agent as a whole; relatedly, insofar as planning (without manipulation or binding of one's future self) assumes such a standpoint, planning may involve a false presupposition. On the other hand, insofar as an agent's evaluative judgments are not changing over time, as in cases of temptation that are cases of impartially benevolent free riding, Bratman's idea that an agent's standpoint might side with her future evaluative judgments (rather than her current evaluative judgments) cannot do any work, since the agent's current and future evaluative judgments coincide.[29]

In relation to the first horn of the dilemma, recall the version of Ulysses' case in which the incredibly sweet singing of the Sirens leads Ulysses to judge the benefits of quickly sailing past the Sirens as not worth the costs of missing this amazing transformative experience, which is hard to deeply appreciate in the

---

[29] See, relatedly, my discussion, in Andreou (2021), of Bratman's one-glass policy case in Bratman (2018). According to the different but related dilemma I pose in relation to that case, "interpreted in one way, the case … is not clearly a case of giving in to temptation (or else not a case that requires the sort of novel contribution Bratman thinks is needed); and interpreted in another way, the case does not raise exactly the challenges Bratman suggests it does, and the challenges it does raise are not directly addressed by the solution Bratman provides" (2021, 8). In this Element, unlike in my 2021 discussion, my challenge is followed by reasoning that suggests that, although we should not adopt Bratman's position, his introduction of the agent's standpoint is a move in the right direction.

abstract (via reflection before or even after the experience). In this case, it seems unwarranted to assume that there is a single standpoint that speaks for Ulysses as a whole. Even if the majority of Ulysses' time slices side with one evaluation, the sorts of special arrangements needed for the majority to speak for the whole do not seem to apply. Notice, in particular, that the case is clearly not, and by its very nature could not be, a case in which each slice has agreed in advance and for the benefit of all to let a voting process reduce their plurality of voices to a single voice that speaks for them all. Nor is it even a case in which all the slices would hypothetically agree if they could. Transformed Ulysses would not; and, as in the case of Homer, it is not to be assumed that the ranking suggested by Ulysses' perspective during the experience that has the potential to prompt reconsideration is in-and-of-itself irrational – that would make the case easier than the philosophical cases of interest.

In relation to the second horn of the dilemma, recall the case of J, who wants to lose enough weight so that he looks about as trim as he was when he got married, but who, in considering, with impartial benevolence, the possibility of a sacrifice by any particular time slice J_n, favors (prospectively, at the time of action, and retrospectively) that J_n get a free ride, since, whatever J's future time slices do, J_n's sacrifice will have no more than a trivial impact on J's appearance. J's taking into account his future evaluative judgments about giving J_n a free ride does nothing but amplify his current evaluative judgment in favor of giving J_n a free ride.

Can an appeal to the agent's standpoint get around this dilemma?

3.5 Rethinking the Agent's Standpoint

According to Bratman, in cases involving shifting evaluative judgments, a planning agent's standpoint will not automatically side with his current evaluative judgment over his future evaluative judgments, except insofar as his current evaluative judgment is appropriately sensitive to the significance of his future evaluative judgments on his current standpoint. For Bratman, this can help make sense of the intuitively plausible idea that, in at least some cases of temptation, it makes sense for an agent to adhere to her prior resolution even if she finds herself with a current evaluative judgment that conflicts with the resolution. Because of the dilemma raised in the previous subsection, I have some doubts about the utility of Bratman's position; but Bratman's introduction of the agent's standpoint is a move in the right direction. In particular, Bratman's insight that an agent's standpoint can transcend her current evaluative judgment (at least insofar as that judgment is not sensitive to what one might describe as meta-considerations) is extremely promising.

Return again to J, whose evaluations are not changing over time. While it is true that, in evaluating, with impartial benevolence, the possibility of a sacrifice by any particular time slice J_n, J favors (prospectively, at the time of action, and retrospectively) that J_n get a free ride, insofar as J is rational, he will also recognize that if he automatically, and without any further grounding considerations, takes an evaluation in favor of granting a free ride as a sufficient basis for doing so, he will grant a free ride to each of his time slices and fail to achieve the goal that he (including all his time slices) is committed to. This meta-consideration – which emerges from taking a holistic perspective and evading separability assumptions that can prompt a series of decisions or moves that suggest a failure to "see the forest for the trees"[30] – allows J to rationally favor *not* acting on his evaluative judgment in favor of granting J_n a free ride. Taking the meta-consideration into account, he can thus rationally favor not giving J_n a free ride. (Indeed, for sufficiently many J_ns, excluding perhaps a few exceptions if they are prompted by a disposition that supports the exceptions *not* becoming the rule, J *must*, upon taking the meta-consideration into account, rationally favor not giving J_n a free ride.)[31] But why take this evaluation rather than the agent's original evaluation to capture the agent's standpoint? A plausible response is that meta-considerations matter and so evaluative judgments that neglect them can be rationally overridden.

If this is right, then we can go even further than Bratman and say that an agent's standpoint can transcend not just her current evaluative judgment but also her past, current, and future evaluative judgments combined when these judgments are not sensitive to meta-considerations that matter in terms of arriving at an evaluation that captures the agent's standpoint. Moreover, we can, in accordance with the two desiderata Bratman is keen on satisfying, allow that (1) there is room for a rational agent experiencing temptation to adhere to a prior plan even if she finds, upon evaluating her options, that she favors abandoning it; and that (2) present evaluation has rational priority, in that "if, when the dust settles, the agent does indeed have a relevant judgment at [the time of action] concerning which alternative would be strictly best at [that time], then, if that agent is functioning rationally, she will opt for that alternative (if she opts for any alternative at all)" (Bratman 2018, 153).

Significantly, the verdicts provided by my transformation of Bratman's position are not the verdicts Bratman's reasoning was meant to support. In

---

[30] Assumptions that can prompt a failure to "see the forest for the trees" are broached again in Section 4.

[31] For some discussion suggesting that the occasional exception can be permissible as appropriately responsive to the force of the meta-consideration if the agent has some disposition that supports the exception(s) *not* becoming the rule, see Andreou (2014b), especially section III.

particular, if, in concretely experiencing what getting in shape commits him to, Homer has a genuine, reasonable change of heart about the value of getting in shape, he will generally not, according to the position defended here, be required to stick with his prior plan, even if, later, when the costs are considered in the abstract, he will revert to favoring getting in shape. Moreover, if Homer does not have a change of heart about the value of getting in shape but, benevolently, favors giving his current self a free ride, there will, according to the position defended here, be rational pressure on him to refrain from taking this evaluative judgment as a sufficient reason to act accordingly, even – or, rather, particularly – if it stems from an impartial benevolence that is shared by his past and future selves. Although these are not the verdicts Bratman's reasoning was meant to support, they are quite plausible and do not, I think, speak against the transformation.

3.6 Deciding How to Decide

Significantly, the meta-consideration in play in the preceding subsection regards the implications of deliberating in a certain way. The agent considers that if he automatically, and without any further grounding considerations, takes an evaluation in favor of granting a free ride as a sufficient basis for doing so, he will grant a free ride to each of his time slices and fail to achieve the goal that he is committed to. In a nutshell, the consideration highlights that reasoning in a certain way is disadvantageous. But a way of reasoning can be disadvantageous without being incorrect. For example, there may be more advantages than disadvantages associated with having an inflated sense of my abilities, but it does not follow that a form of reasoning that does not skew my sense of my abilities is incorrect. This suggests that how best to reason is not a matter to be settled by considering the pragmatic advantages and disadvantages of various ways of reasoning; it is a question settled by theoretical considerations regarding what makes for good reasoning. To borrow from David Velleman, "how [best] to decide is something we discover rather than decide [on the basis of practical considerations]" (2000, 221). According to Velleman, to suggest otherwise is to steer into a serious methodological problem, since "if how to conceive of practical reasoning is itself a practical question ... then we shall have no conception of how to answer the question until we have already answered it. We shall therefore find ourselves either unable to answer the question at all or forced to answer it arbitrarily" (2000, 229). But then isn't there something problematic about J's revising his evaluative judgment regarding granting J_n a free ride on the basis of a consideration regarding acting on evaluative judgments of this sort?

Here, it might be replied that, even if – and this is a big if – Velleman is right in insisting that how to deliberate well when it comes to deciding what to do is a "theoretical matter," J's reasoning need not be misguided. For, it can be a theoretical truth about practical reasoning that a mode of deliberation that is self-defeating is worse than an equally accurate and coherent mode of deliberation that is not self-defeating. There is certainly room for theories of practical reasoning that, without too crudely connecting practical reasoning with practical success, postulate a connection that suggests that it is not just disadvantageous but "mistaken to treat rational deliberation as self-defeating if a non-self-defeating account is available" (Gauthier 1994, 702). Indeed, although Velleman takes it that David Gauthier's "conception of practical reason is commended to the agent by the practical considerations about the benefits of holding it" (Velleman 2000, 224), Gauthier's theory, which will be discussed shortly, can be interpreted as embracing the idea that there is an objective criterion for success that is a matter of theoretical discovery rather than decision. The criterion, according to Gauthier's metaethical theorizing (in, for example, Gauthier 1991), is, roughly put, the satisfaction of one's concerns; and this criterion is used to discover (rather than decide on) correct deliberative principles, which in turn determine our reasons for action. For Gauthier, his position is justified in light of "our present world view," which rejects the idea that "the world [is] purposively ordered" but recognizes that agents have preferences that preserve the relevance of preference-centered forms of justification (1991, 16). In any case, whether or not Gauthier's theory is correct – and, though I will say quite a bit more about it in what follows, I do *not* mean to suggest that it is correct – we can and should embrace the related but relatively modest suggestion that meta-considerations raise theoretically significant complications in relation to the question of what is involved in deliberating well; moreover, recognizing the theoretical significance of meta-considerations is compatible with the idea that how to deliberate well is a "theoretical matter." As such, it is hasty to dismiss J – or, more specifically, J's revising his evaluative judgment concerning granting J_n a free ride on the basis of a consideration regarding acting on evaluative judgments of this sort – as misguidedly proceeding in a way that is not theoretically grounded.

3.7 Actions and Deliberative Procedures

Although I have reservations about Gauthier's theory, particularly given some complications that I will discuss in Section 4, it is, I think, ingenious and very much worth exploring. His defense of resoluteness incorporates the intriguing suggestion that, even if what matters from the point of view of rationality is how well an agent serves her preferences, whether an agent has proceeded rationally in some scenario should be judged not in terms of whether she takes the *action* that best serves her preferences but in terms of whether her *deliberative procedure* best serves her preferences (Gauthier 1994). Now it might seem safe to assume that the deliberative procedure that best serves an agent's preferences is precisely the deliberative procedure that prompts her to invariably opt for the action that best serves her preferences, and so there is no room for divergence between these two possible forms of assessment; but this assumption has been critiqued as hasty. Given the possibility of Prisoner's Dilemma situations and closely related dilemmas, it has been argued that agents who are somewhat translucent, in that how they deliberate "affects the expectations of their fellows about what they will do," are served better by a deliberative procedure that calls for resoluteness in certain cases than by a deliberative procedure that invariably calls for selecting the action that best serves one's preferences (Gauthier 1994, 16).

Call the agent who invariably selects the action that best serves her concerns a "straightforward maximizer" and consider the following situation:

> My crops will be ready for harvesting next week, yours a fortnight hence. Each of us will do better if we harvest together than if we harvest alone. [But, once I receive your help, helping you will be a pure cost to me.] You will help me next week if you expect that in return I shall help you in a fortnight . . . . [If, however, we are both straightforward maximizers,] you know that I would not return your help, and being no sucker, will therefore leave me to harvest my crops alone. Neither of us will assist the other, and so each of us will do worse than need be. We shall fail to gain the potential benefits of cooperation. (Gauthier 1994, 692)

Agents whose deliberative procedure prompts them to resolutely stick to cooperative plans will do better. For then the agent who will receive help first can credibly assure the other that she will do her part, even though she has nothing to gain by following through after the other has helped.

As suggested by Gauthier's description of the farming case, given agents that are translucent, an agent who makes false assurances will not do better than one who makes genuine assurances since the insincerity of the former will not go undetected. If fickleness is also detectable, translucency can also work against the agent who provides a genuine assurance but, due to her fickleness, characteristically loses her resolve when the time for action arrives. For, not being "suckers," potential cooperators will avoid her too.

3.8 Indirect Evaluation of Actions

While it is natural to think of the resolute agent as showing restraint and the straightforward maximizer as unrestrained, it is worth emphasizing that both can be seen as equally committed to maximizing (insofar as maximizing is possible); it's just that the straightforward maximizer maximizes at the level of actions and the resolute agent maximizes at the level of deliberative procedures. Insofar as the deliberative procedure that best serves one's concerns is not the procedure that tells one to invariably choose the action that best serves one's concerns, the two forms of maximization will sometimes come apart. And, assuming "that the standards of rational advisability can be accepted without inconsistency," one cannot be required to adhere to both forms of maximization (Andreou 2018b). Either rationality will require that one maximize at the level of deliberative procedures and assess actions indirectly, in terms of whether they are called for by the deliberative procedure that best serves one's preferences (rather than in terms of whether the actions themselves best serve one's preferences), or else rationality will require that one maximize at the level of actions and assess deliberative procedures indirectly, in terms of whether they call for actions that best serve one's preferences (rather than in terms of whether the deliberative procedures themselves best serves one's preferences). The standard approach is to assess actions directly; but, insofar as what matters is serving one's preferences well, having the best deliberative procedure is better than invariably choosing the best actions. For, given the possibility of Prisoner's Dilemma situations, and closely related dilemmas, the latter turns out to be counterproductive (in terms of achieving what matters). This suggests that actions are better assessed indirectly (but see Section 4 for a more nuanced discussion of the apparent and arguably oversimplified contrast between evaluating actions directly and evaluating deliberative procedures).[32]

3.9 Self-Control, Quasi-Resoluteness, and Strict Resoluteness

Given intrapersonal free-rider cases like the retirement savings case and the dieting case discussed above, it seems plausible to maintain that agents whose deliberative procedure prompts them to stick to their self-control plans do better than agents who invariably follow their preferences. But there are some interesting complications to consider.

Return to J's case, in which J aims to diet in order to impact his appearance, but let's leave open the possibility that J is capable of resolutely sticking to a self-control plan, and suppose J adopts the plan to have a tasty treat once a week. While it seems true that J is better off as a resolute chooser than as

---

[32] See also Thompson (2008, part 3) for some interesting nuanced discussion concerning the connection between the idea that the rational evaluation of actions should be indirect and "practice versions of utilitarianism."

a straightforward maximizer, it also seems true that it would be even more advantageous for J if he was disposed to make the occasional exception to his self-control plan. Of course, if the exceptions became the rule, he would fail to achieve his goal of losing weight, and so he'd fare badly if he was not disposed to be at least quasi-resolute, where quasi-resoluteness would require that he not deviate too far from his original plan. This might be achieved by a disposition in which he is willing to stray from his original plan here and there but gets increasingly reluctant to stray as he gets further and further from his original anchor point (in this case, fifty-two treats a year).[33]

This sounds plausible if J's disposition to allow for a few free rides is motivated by benevolence, but what if J's time slices are each partial to themselves, and so are not attracted by a few exceptions here and there, but favor a single exception for themselves? In this case, the form of quasi-resoluteness that best serves each time slice differs: each J_n seems to be best served by the deliberative procedure that calls for resoluteness except at time n. If, however, how each time slice deliberates affects the expectations of other time slices, this deliberative procedure may prompt other time slices (in particular, earlier time slices) to seek to constrain rather than cooperate with J_n, and so the one-exception-for-me deliberative procedure might not be as advantageous as it initially seems. An earlier time slice, J_m, that anticipates that J_n will not be resolute at time n may, being "no sucker," predictably incur a cost that leaves both J_m and J_n poorer to ensure that J_n is precommitted to J_m's plan. In this case, both J_m and J_n would do better if J_n was disposed to be strictly resolute (i.e., resolute without exception).

Importantly, the idea that J_n's adhering to J_m's plan qualifies as resolutely following through on his *own* prior plan assumes that J is unified enough to figure as a continuing self (which suggests that J_n and J_m are not properly understood, modeled, or treated as completely separate agents).[34] Without sufficient unity, talk of resoluteness and self-control are misplaced. The case in which J_n and J_m discount future utility, but share a long-term goal, falls between the case in which J_n and J_m are clearly unified by a fully shared and impartially pursued aim, and the case in which J_n and J_m are completely at odds due to a sharp divergence in their views regarding what matters and what is worth pursuing (as are, on one interpretation, earlier Ulysses and later Ulysses).

---

[33] For related discussion concerning the possibly of plans providing anchor points, see Andreou (2014b).

[34] See Thoma (2018, 41), who, in a critique of one way of interpreting McClennen (1990, 1998) on resoluteness, emphasizes that, without sufficient unity, so-called resoluteness requires an agent to "act on a resolution that she did not make herself."

3.10 Autonomous Benefit Cases

J will not achieve his goal of losing weight if he invariably abandons his plans to show restraint at the time of action. His plans to show restraint are beneficial only if they are not altogether disregarded. There are, however, cases in which an agent's plans to show restraint are in and of themselves beneficial, regardless of whether they are acted on. Such cases qualify as *autonomous benefit cases*. In autonomous benefit cases, an agent benefits from forming a certain intention whether or not she ends up following through on her intention. The rationality of resoluteness in such cases is even more controversial than in cases like J's; but for those sympathetic with Gauthier's theory, acceptance of the rationality of such resoluteness is in order. Consider, to illustrate with a particularly famous case of the relevant sort that I will return to in Section 4, Gregory Kavka's toxin case. As Kavka's describes the case,

> an eccentric billionaire ... places before you a vial of toxin .... If you drink [the toxin], [it] will make you painfully ill for a day, but will not threaten your life or have any lasting effects .... The billionaire will pay you one million dollars tomorrow morning if, at midnight tonight, you intend to drink the toxin tomorrow afternoon .... You need not drink the toxin to receive the money; in fact, the money will already be in your bank account hours before the time for drinking it arrives, if you succeed .... [The] arrangement of ... external incentives is ruled out, as are such alternative gimmicks as hiring a hypnotist to implant the intention ... (Kavka 1983, 33–34)

If rationality calls for straightforward maximization, then a rational agent will not be able to gain the million. For, when the time for action arrives, drinking the toxin will figure as a pure cost, and so a rational agent will have no reason to drink the toxin and a strong reason not to (assuming rationality calls for straightforward maximization); she will thus not drink the toxin. And given that, as a rational agent, she can (assuming she is not shortsighted) anticipate this, she will not be able to form the intention to drink the toxin since she cannot intend to do what she knows she will not do. The million will thus not be placed in her account.

For a rational agent to gain the million, rationality must, it seems, allow for resolute choice in autonomous benefit cases. Does it? Well, if rationality prompts one to follow the deliberative procedure that best serves one's concerns – and this remains, of course, a big if, even if one accepts the relatively modest suggestion that meta-considerations matter and so evaluative judgments that neglect them can be rationally overridden – then the answer seems to be "yes." For, given the agent's translucency, she does better with a deliberative procedure that prompts her to drink the toxin than with a deliberative procedure that prohibits her from drinking the toxin. Only with a deliberative procedure of the former sort is there nothing standing in the way of a rational agent's forming the intention to drink the toxin and so nothing standing in the way of her gaining the million.[35]

Notably, even if gimmicks like hiring a hypnotist to implant the intention were allowed, and so the straightforward maximizer could gain the million, he would have to incur a cost a resolute agent could avoid by simply resolving to drink the toxin.

3.11 Conclusion

Resoluteness involves a willingness to stick to a plan even if one believes that what the plan calls for conflicts with one's current preferences or would conflict with one's current preferences if one were to disengage from one's previous decision and reconsider things from one's current perspective. This section has focused on whether resoluteness is a genuine possibility for a rational agent. We have looked at arguments that it is. These arguments – some of which seem promising, but all of which are controversial given the skepticism about resoluteness that figures as standard in decision theory – suggest that incurring costs to precommit to an option by penalizing or eliminating alternatives may be a needlessly roundabout route to solving dilemmas in which certain benefits of cooperation or self-control cannot be realized without restraint. For, given the possibility of rational resoluteness, rational agents can reliably resolve to adhere to a cooperative or self-controlled course and follow through; precommitment devices might then only be needed to compensate for irrational irresoluteness.

4 Taking Extended Agents Seriously

4.1 Introduction

This section delves into some complications concerning the nature of actions and the nature of intentions that I have so far been abstracting from. I here follow, with some condensing, synthesizing, and adjusted illustrations suited to fit my current purposes, selections from two strands of my prior work.[36] The complications that I focus on are tied to the fact that correctly evaluating what an agent is doing at a particular point in time requires recognizing what the agent is doing at that point in time, and this is not a trivial matter, since what an

---

[35] See Gauthier (1994).

[36] See Andreou (2014a), particularly in relation to subsections 4.2–4.5, and Andreou (2016), particularly in relation to subsections 4.6–4.9. In light of this general acknowledgment, I will refrain from repeatedly referencing the papers and stick to referencing only direct quotations.

agent is doing *at* a particular point in time is normally not contained *in* that point in time. As I will explain, once this is recognized, certain assumptions and distinctions that are routinely taken for granted emerge as questionable. To echo an aside from Section 3, it is important to take a holistic perspective and evade assumptions that can prompt a failure to "see the forest for the trees."

4.2 Doings in Progress

Actions, at least ones that can be completed, unfold over time. Walking to school, crossing the street, taking a step, and even moving one's foot an inch forward are not completed instantaneously; still, all of these doings may be in progress at some point in time t^*. Interestingly, these doings can qualify as in progress at t^* even if they are never completed because they are interrupted by, say, a speeding bus.[37] As such, though I do not qualify as, say, having crossed the street until this doing in progress is completed, I do qualify as crossing the street at every point in time at which the doing is underway. Even if a bus interrupts my progress by hitting me a fraction of a second after I begin crossing the street, I was still, right before being hit, crossing the street. Though I was closer to completing the doing in progress of taking a step, it is no less true that I was crossing the street than that I was taking a step; by hypothesis, both doings were in progress – via the exact same motions – before being tragically interrupted.[38]

Now forget about the bus, which never really hit me, and suppose I have a snapshot of me at t^* on 1st Avenue. You ask what I was doing when the snapshot was taken. Because I was performing a temporally extended action, the answer is not any doing that could be contained in t^*. Instead, the answer will cite the doings that were in progress at t^*, which will, we can suppose, include: moving my foot an inch forward; taking a step; crossing the street; and so on. Notably, the answers would be the same even if I had, not a snapshot of me at t^*, but a one-second videoclip and your question was about what I was doing when the videoclip was taken. In this case, there might be some doing contained in the clip, perhaps the doing of moving my

---

[37] See Anscombe (1963, §23), Thompson (2008, part 2), and Tenenbaum (2020) for some important action-theoretic contributions that emphasize, rather than abstracting from, doings in progress and their philosophically interesting features.

[38] The suggestion that what I am doing at a certain time may be describable as "taking a step" and "crossing the street" might be reminiscent of Davidson's famous switch-flipping example, in which what I doing at a certain time is describable as "flipping a switch" and "alerting a prowler to the fact that I am home"; but Davidson's two descriptions highlight the fact that "reasons may rationalize what someone does when it is described in one way and not when it is described in another" (Davidson 2001, 5), whereas the two descriptions "taking a step" and "crossing the street" highlight the possibility of overlapping actions in progress. An example that fits more neatly with Davidson's point figures in subsection 4.3.

foot an inch forward; but it would still be true that what I was doing when the videoclip was taken was moving my foot an inch forward, taking a step, crossing the street, etc., all via the exact same motion. Now suppose that it was rationally impermissible for me to be crossing the street when the videoclip was taken because crossing the street conflicted with some more important aim of mine. Then I would be rationally criticizable at that time even if, as luck would have it, my crossing the street was interrupted (by some unexpected but non-fatal incident) as soon as the videorecorder was stopped, and I never got any further than moving my foot an inch forward. Since, in the context, what I was (in the process of) doing in moving my foot an inch forward was also describable as crossing the street, I didn't need to get any further to be criticizable. While I might not have been criticizable if I was merely moving my foot an inch forward, I do not count as merely moving my foot an inch forward if my moving my foot an inch forward is, in the context at hand, also describable as my crossing the street.

4.3 Doings, Dispositions, and Dynamics

The logic of things in progress is not limited to intentional actions (Anscombe 1963, §23; Thompson 2008, 126). To take a variation on a case provided by Michael Thompson that I have used before, consider a "tomato [that] was ripening on a vine but [that] never actually ripened because an explosion occurred that almost instantly vaporized everything at ground zero, including the tomato" (Andreou 2014a, 218). In this case, the ripening of the tomato is in progress even though the tomato never ends up having ripened.

Since something (or someone) can be X-ing even if it (or one) never ends up having X-ed, the logic of something in progress is tied to the notion of a natural default: the natural default, if B is X-ing, is that, in due course, B will have X-ed. This natural default must be tied to dispositions or dynamics that, barring interruption, bring it about.

In the case of doings in progress, natural defaults are often tied to intentions as follows: If I intend to X, then the natural default is that, in due course, I will have X-ed. If I don't X, something must have interrupted the progression that was initiated by my intention – e.g., a speeding bus, a lapse of memory, or a change of mind. But, notably, I need not intend to X or be intentionally X-ing for it to be a natural default that, in due course, I will have X-ed. For instance, if I intend to cross the street, and, in the circumstances, crossing the street will ruin my sneakers, then, even if I am unaware of this side-effect and am not intentionally ruining my sneakers, it is a natural default that, in due course, I will have ruined my sneakers; for it is a natural default that, in due course, I will have crossed the street and thus ruined my sneakers.[39] It is thus true not only that I am crossing the street but also that I am ruining my sneakers. Similarly, if I am disposed to cross at this crosswalk every morning, which, unbeknownst to me, is coated with an odorless but easily disturbed and extremely toxic chemical that is harmful given repeated or sustained exposure, then, not only am I crossing the street and taking my usual route to work, I am also, perhaps, damaging my brain in that, without a change in disposition or circumstances, I will, in due course, suffer irremediable cognitive impairment.

4.4 Impartially Benevolent Free Riding Revisited

The fact that what an agent is doing *at* a particular point in time is normally not contained *in* that point in time raises some interesting complications in relation to cases of impartially benevolent free riding, understood as cases of free riding motivated by impartial benevolence. Recall that in such cases, it is tempting to reason as follows: a contribution by J_n (where J_n is some self or time slice) will have no more than a trivial impact in relation to the benevolent goal at stake (in that this particular potential contribution is not make or break in terms of the achievement of the goal); but making the contribution involves a genuine sacrifice; so it is preferable that J_n refrain from contributing. The problem, of course, is that there is nothing distinctive about J_n and so the sort of benevolent thinking under consideration can, like free riding motivated by partiality, result in the important goal never being met. As will become apparent, some of the previously discussed points about doings in progress suggest that this apparent dilemma abstracts from certain complications related to action individuation. If these complications are taken into account, it becomes clear that *not* all of the doings (or omissions) occurring at points on the way to failure in relation to the goal at stake are at most trivially detrimental relative to the goal.

Consider an intrapersonal case in which an agent fails to achieve a long-term goal because he keeps benevolently excusing his current self from taking on a substantial burden for the sake of a trivial contribution to the long-term goal. Take the case of S, who enjoys eating treats but also wants to remain fashionably slim. Suppose that S is correct in supposing that each instance of culinary indulgence will have at most a tiny effect on his appearance – regardless of how he currently looks, consuming one more treat will make no more than a trivial difference. Suppose further that, knowing that consuming one more

---

[39] For Bratman's famous but importantly different sneaker example and his associated discussion regarding when a side effect such as ruining one's sneakers might count as intentional, see Bratman (1987, chapter 8, section 8.5). My example, like Davidson's previously mentioned switch-flipping example (see note 38), considers a scenario in which the agent is not aware of an important alternative description of what he is doing.

treat will have at most a tiny effect on his appearance, S accepts treats as they are offered to him and ends up having "ruined" his figure (relative to the standard he is committed to). (For convenience, I won't keep including the scare quotes and parenthetical qualification included in the preceding sentence; they will henceforth remain implicit.)

For any particular treat he is offered, it seems preferable, relative to S's concerns, for him to have that treat; relatedly, it might seem like, despite his going astray, at no point along the way does S do anything that is detrimental relative to his concerns – to the contrary, at each point he is doing what best serves his concerns. But is this right? To get to the bottom of this, we need to pinpoint what S is doing at each point along the way, and this is not a trivial matter. For recall that what S is doing *at* a particular point in time is normally not contained *in* that point in time, and so we'll need to pick out all the doings in progress and consider whether any of them are detrimental relative to his concerns. Suppose a snapshot of S at some point in time along the way reveals S's mouth opened around a half-eaten brownie. The doings in progress obviously include S's moving his jaw and S's eating a brownie, but they can also include S's ruining his figure. What doings are in progress depends on the dispositions and dynamics that are in place and that generate natural defaults that support the ascription of certain doings in progress. If the dispositions and dynamics that are in place are such that, barring interruption, S's figure will, in due course, be ruined, then S is ruining his figure. The relevant dispositions and dynamics might include S's disposition to accept treats he is offered with the thought "well, this one little treat won't make or break my chance of staying fashionably slim," or without any thought at all and only the reaction "yum." If these dispositions are in place and S is ruining his figure at the point in time that the supposed snapshot is taken, then it is clearly not the case that what he is doing at that point in time has only a trivial impact in relation to his goal of remaining slim. To achieve his goal, he must desist from ruining his figure. There may be ways of doing this that are consistent with his continuing to eat the brownie. He may, for example, find a way to precommit to this brownie being his only brownie this year. But then he has solved his problem and it is, other things equal, rational for him to eat this brownie, since, in this situation, his current doings really will have no more than a trivial impact in relation to his goal. If, however, S proceeds to eat the brownie without any change in circumstance or disposition, then, regardless of what excuses S makes to himself, he is still, while eating the brownie, engaged in the doing in progress of ruining his figure. His current doing is thus not plausibly understood as an instance of harmless free riding. Properly understood, his doing in progress is detrimental (relative to his end of remaining fashionably slim), even if he is motivated by a naive benevolence toward each of his time slices. Of course, if his doing in progress is interrupted, the detrimental natural consequence of his doing in progress may never be realized because his doing in progress is never completed; but, the expected harm of his doing in progress would then be evaded by luck, and so he would remain rationally criticizable for having proceeded.

4.5 Action Individuation and Units of Agency

The complication raised in the preceding subsection concerning action individuation is closely related to a complication concerning units of agency. We've seen that, given a snapshot at time t*, the question of what was going on when the snapshot was taken is not to be found by trying to find a doing contained in the point in time t*. The snapshot may be of S eating a brownie at t* even if – to quote Thompson (2008, 126) – S's eating a brownie "reaches beyond" t*. Given that temporally extended actions require temporally extended agents, it is misguided to think about what was going on when the snapshot was taken as executed by a non-temporally extended agent S*. Being temporally extended, any doing going on at t* must be attributable to an agent that endures for more than that single point in time. In the brownie case, it is natural to attribute the doings in progress to S, who persists for the duration of the relevant doings (which include jaw-moving, brownie-eating, and figure-ruining), assuming they are not interrupted. Once it is recognized that a doing at t* will normally reach beyond t* and be attributable to an entity sufficiently temporally extended to carry out the doing, it becomes clear that, as with figuring out what doings are going on at t*, figuring out to whom to attribute the doings at t* is not a matter of looking for entities in t*.

This has interesting implications for interpersonal doings in progress. Consider, for example, that

> we talk not only about individuals doing things, but also about groups of individuals doing things, where these things might be such that they could not or just would not be accomplished by any individual in the group working solo. Take a case in which we are making a kite. This can figure as a collective doing in progress. Barring rerouting or interruption, a collective doing in progress will be completed in due course by the collective. As in the individual case, what the collective is doing *at* this moment need not be the sort of thing that can fit *in* this moment . . .. For example, we can be making a kite at this moment, even if the only contributory bit of action that can be found *in* this moment is my dropping a glob of glue on a stick. Note that my dropping a glob of glue on a stick is "smaller" than the collective doing in progress occurring *at* this moment in two ways: dropping a glob of glue on a stick is smaller than making a kite; and the step-taker – me . . . – is smaller than we. Still, it is true not only that *I* . . . am *dropping a glob of glue on a stick* and that

I ... am constructing a wooden cross with two sticks that my partner just measured and cut, but also that *we* are *making a kite*. (Andreou 2014a, 217)

If this idea is considered in relation to interpersonal cases of free riding motivated by impartial benevolence of the sort that I consider in Section 1, and it is kept in mind that what doings are in progress depends on the dispositions and dynamics that are in place and that generate natural defaults that support the ascription of certain doings in progress, we can see that, as in intrapersonal cases, some of the doings occurring at various points on the way to failure in relation to the goal at stake are actually non-trivially detrimental in relation to the goal.

Return to the case introduced in subsection 1.7 of a unified collective that "values a healthy community, values luxuries whose production or use promotes a carcinogenic environment, and believes [correctly] that if it does not curb its consumption, the health of the community will be seriously damaged"; and suppose that the collective "opts for a high level of consumption month after month, [and this results in] the health of the community [being] seriously damaged" (Andreou 2006a, 104). While it might seem like each instance of luxury consumption, and so each doing along the way, has no more than a trivial impact in relation to the community's goal because it "will not take the community's members from a state of decent health to a state of poor health" (Andreou 2006a, 104), this overlooks certain doings in progress. If the dispositions and dynamics that are in place are such that, barring interruption, the health of the community's members will be seriously damaged by their luxury consumption, then, for each point in time t* at which an individual, say B, is engaged in luxury consumption, one of the doings in progress at that time is "we are damaging the health of the community." The relevant dispositions and dynamics might include each member's disposition to proceed with certain rationalizations in mind, or without thought and simply in line with a certain routine or habit. Importantly, and as emphasized in the toxic chemical brain damage case described above, a detrimental doing in progress need not be intentional under the description that qualifies it as detrimental. Just as I can, given certain dispositions, dynamics, and natural defaults, be damaging my brain without coordinating on doing so or being guided by any intention that is thought to involve doing so, we can, given certain dispositions, dynamics, and natural defaults, be damaging our health without coordinating on doing so or being guided by any intention that is thought to involve doing so. Of course, if we recognize or should recognize that some damage is underway via some doing in progress, we might be culpable for failing to disengage from the doing in progress by, say, coordinating on and precommitting to a better course.

4.6 Actions and Deliberative Frameworks

Although X-ing may figure as a doing in progress even if no one is guided by any objective that involves X-ing, when X-ing is intentional, the dispositions that make what is going on qualify as X-ing include certain deliberative dispositions. As I will explain, via a condensed version of some of my reasoning in Andreou (2016), this suggests that "even the most direct evaluation of intentional actions involves the evaluation of different ways of deliberating about what to do" (625); and this in turn suggests that the contrast between evaluating actions and evaluating deliberative procedures, which was reviewed in Section 3 (on resoluteness) may be oversimplified.[40]

An agent does not count as intentionally X-ing unless her deliberative framework (which determines how she reasons in light of certain beliefs and considerations) includes certain features. Suppose, for example, that A takes it that Y-ing is necessary for X-ing and, more generally, for anything that involves X-ing. Then, tangential hedging aside, unless this consideration settles for A the question of whether to Y, A does not qualify as intentionally X-ing. If, for instance, A believes that, to get to grandma's or do anything that involves getting to grandma's, she must traverse the forest, and yet this consideration does not settle for her the question of whether to traverse the forest, then she is not (intentionally) going to grandma's.

An agent's deliberative framework changes over time depending on what she is doing. If A is intentionally going to grandma's, she will take the consideration that she must traverse the forest to get to grandma's or do anything that involves getting to grandma's as settling the question of whether to traverse the forest. If, however, she is intentionally going to the store to buy a new hoodie, the consideration that she must traverse the forest to get to grandma's will not settle anything (assuming going to the store to buy a new hoodie does not involve getting to grandma's). An agent's deliberative framework will also, however, normally include a stable core. For example, an agent that values being a good grandchild and believes that calling grandma daily is essential for being a good grandchild may, as a stable feature of her deliberative framework, take the consideration that calling grandma daily is essential for being a good grandchild as settling the question of whether to call grandma daily. Notably, the stable core of an agent's deliberative framework may include general deliberative proced-ures or components of such procedures. For instance, the stable core of an agent's deliberative framework might be such that, tangential qualifications

---

[40] My reasoning in Andreou (2016) builds on some points I make in Andreou (2006b, 2009), which include some examples that are similar to those included later in the text.

aside, the agent takes considerations of the form "X-ing is required as part of keeping my word" as settling the question of whether to X.

Insofar as intentionally X-ing involves integrating particular constraints into one's deliberative framework, even a direct evaluation of intentionally X-ing involves an evaluation of integrating particular constraints into one's deliberative framework. Suppose, for example, that A is (intentionally) X-ing and, recognizing that Y-ing is necessary for X-ing and, more generally, for anything that involves X-ing, takes this consideration as settling the question of whether to Y. Accepting that A's X-ing is rational involves accepting the rationality of A's adopting and deliberating in accordance with a deliberative framework that takes the consideration that Y-ing is necessary for X-ing and, more generally, for anything that involves X-ing as settling the question of whether to Y. There is thus something off base about the question of whether to apply the criterion of evaluation to actions or instead to deliberative frameworks since there is no way to disentangle (intentionally) X-ing from deliberating in accordance with a deliberative framework that is constrained accordingly.

4.7 Autonomous Benefit Cases and Resoluteness Revisited

And yet, there seem to be cases in which selecting the maximizing action and following the maximizing deliberative procedure diverge. Return to Kavka's toxin case, discussed in section 3.10, in which an eccentric billionaire will "pay you one million dollars tomorrow morning if, at midnight tonight, you intend to drink the toxin tomorrow afternoon" (Kavka 1983, 33). You do not actually have to drink the toxin to get the million. The money will be deposited into your account before the time the toxin is available arrives. According to Gauthier's reasoning, a straightforward maximizer who evaluates actions directly will not be able to gain the million dollars; for, she knows that she will not drink the toxin when the opportunity arises, since drinking the toxin is a pure cost. But an agent who evaluates deliberative procedures will see that a procedure that calls for resoluteness in cases like the toxin case is better, in terms of serving her concerns well, than one that invariably calls for selecting the action that best serves her concerns. Such an agent can form the intention to drink the toxin knowing she will resolutely follow through. In this case, it seems like one's verdict about the rationality of drinking the toxin will depend on whether one directly evaluates the action of drinking the toxin or instead evaluates the deliberative framework or procedure that calls for resoluteness and then selects the action that accords with this procedure. But this conclusion is hasty.

Suppose you have somehow managed to form the intention to drink the toxin (perhaps because you anticipated resolutely following through) and are now faced with the toxin. It occurs to you to reconsider your intention. You ask yourself if you should drink the toxin, given that you formed the intention to do so and thus received the million dollars, or should instead abandon your intention. If you opt for the former, you will be taking the consideration that "drinking the toxin is required to carry out an intention that it was advantageous for me to form" as settling the question of whether to drink the toxin. Directly evaluating drinking the toxin, in the relevant context, is thus inextricably tied to evaluating being resolute. If, on the one hand, you will not benefit from remaining resolute (even though you benefited from being resolute before), then neither drinking the toxin nor remaining resolute gets a positive evaluation. If, on the other hand, you will benefit from remaining resolute and you cannot remain resolute unless you take the consideration that "drinking the toxin is required to carry out an intention that it was advantageous for me to form" as settling the question of whether to drink the toxin, and so drink it, then both drinking the toxin and remaining resolute get a positive evaluation. Notably, Gauthier specifically allows that "the fully rational being is able to reflect on his standard of deliberation, and to change that standard in the light of reflection" (Gauthier 1986, 183). Were this not possible, Gauthier's argument could not convince a straightforward maximizer to be resolute instead.

4.8 On-the-Whole Evaluations versus Evaluations through Time

It might be objected that the preceding reasoning assumes that the best deliberative procedure (even assuming it is comprehensive) can vary over time. But perhaps deliberative procedures are to be compared on the assumption that each is used consistently over time, in which case "best" is to be read as "best on the whole." So understood, the best deliberative procedure calls for resoluteness in toxin type cases.

But just as one can insist on evaluating deliberative procedures "on the whole" rather than through time, one can also insist on evaluating (temporally extended courses of) action "on the whole" rather than through time, with "the phases of an action or course of action . . . united by the deliberative constraints that would have to be in play for each phase to count as directed toward the same end or object" (Andreou 2016, 627); and, so long as evaluation is always of wholes, there won't be conflicting verdicts. Notice, for example, that forming the intention to drink the toxin at time t and then drinking it at t qualify as part of a united whole:

> Throughout the time the agent intends to drink the toxin (preparing the way by, at a minimum, avoiding conflicting engagements), embarks on drinking it (lifting it to his lips), and follows through (swallowing the nasty stuff), the

> agent's deliberation is constrained by the same end or object – he is navigating himself with an eye to drinking the toxin at time t, and is thus pursuing the same (course of) action.[41] Whether time t has arrived or still lies ahead, the agent takes considerations of the form "X-ing is necessary for drinking the toxin at time t" as settling the question of whether to X. This framework unites the phases of the agent's navigating himself with an eye to drinking the toxin at time t. (Andreou 2016, 634)

And, judged as a whole, this course of action is better than the course of action in which one refrains from forming the intention to drink the toxin and does not drink it. Importantly, forming the intention to drink the toxin and then not drinking it does not count as a unified course of action but as switching courses; and so, as long as one sticks to the evaluation of whole courses of action, forming the intention to drink the toxin and drinking it qualifies as the best course of action.

The moral, in short, is that, so long as actions and deliberative procedures are evaluated in the same way, either both as wholes or, alternatively, both through time, one will not get conflicting verdicts regarding the best alternative.

4.9 The Million-Dollar Question

I suggested in the last subsection that intending to Z and then (following through and) intentionally Z-ing are united in the sense that an agent qualifies as intending to Z and then intentionally Z-ing only if, throughout the relevant time frame, she takes considerations of the form "X-ing is necessary for Z-ing" as settling the question of whether to X. Also worth noting is that the natural default of intending to Z and of intentionally Z-ing is that one will, in due course and barring interruption, have Z-ed. Intending to Z is thus very similar to the various phases of Z-ing (especially phases in which one is not actively doing anything but simply waiting for the next cue, as for example, when one is waiting for the oven to finish preheating after one has mixed the batter while making a cake).[42] Given this unity between intending to Z and then intentionally Z-ing, toxin-like cases can be constructed in which the benefit one stands to gain is not tied to intending to perform some action in the future but to some early phase of the action. Consider the following case:

> Suppose an action theorist with a large grant offers an agent the following deal: she will get a million dollars if, in five minutes from now, she is

---

[41] For discussion of some closely related ideas, see Bratman (1987), Thompson (2008, part 2), Ferrero (2017), and Tenenbaum (2020).

[42] For a detailed discussion regarding "gappy" actions that features the "gappy" action of making a cake, see Tenenbaum (2020). Notably, once the cake is in the oven, it can still be true that I am making a cake, even if, to quote Thompson (2008, 99), "at the moment (as we say), I am playing cards or napping."

intentionally going to her office. Suppose the trip would take 20 minutes and the agent knows that the first half of the trip would be no trouble but the second half of the trip would involve stressful driving through construction. The action theorist makes it clear that the agent will get the million dollars in five minutes if she is then going to her office and the money will not be revoked after that even if she never actually goes to her office (i.e., she never completes her action-in-progress). The rest of the details of the case are such that, by hypothesis, the potential office-goer does best if, in five minutes, she is going to her office but, soon thereafter, she is giving up and turning back. (Andreou 2016, 635)

Although the agent does best if, in five minutes from now, she is going to her office, but then, shortly thereafter, she changes her mind and turns back, this is not a unified course of action; and, indeed, the agent does not count as going to her office if she is planning on turning back before she arrives. She is heading towards her office; but that is not the same thing and it does not suffice to get her the million dollars. As in the toxin case, it looks like the rational agent can get the million dollars only if it is rational to evaluate things on the whole rather than through time. Whether it is remains the million-dollar question.

4.10 Conclusion

This section has focused on some complications concerning the nature of actions and the nature of intentions that are easily overlooked. The complications are tied to the fact that correctly evaluating what an agent is doing at a particular point in time requires recognizing what the agent is doing at that point in time. Since what an agent is doing *at* a particular point in time is normally not contained *in* that point in time, this is not a trivial matter; it requires recognizing what dispositions, dynamics, and defaults are in play. In light of the complications raised in this section of the Element, I revisited and revised some earlier suggestions regarding benevolent free riding, autonomous benefit cases, and resoluteness. I ended by contrasting on-the-whole evaluations and evaluations through time, and by posing the related "million-dollar question": Is it rational to evaluate things on the whole or though time?

Conclusion

This Element has focused on debates concerning the interaction between cooperation, commitment, and control. Though commitment might seem either redundant or irrational, depending on whether the course committed to fits or does not fit with what one would have reason to do apart from the commitment, there are a variety of interesting positions that have been developed that suggest that the ability to commit to a dispreferred alternative is necessary to reap the benefits of cooperation or self-control.

Section 1 discussed interpersonal and intrapersonal Prisoner's Dilemma situations, and the possibility of a set of unrestrained choices adding up in a way that is problematic relative to the concerns of the choosers involved. I reviewed some key moves and refinements in debates regarding Prisoner's Dilemma situations with an eye to providing an illuminating big-picture view of the terrain that is relevant for debates regarding commitment, cooperation, and control. I also developed, with novel precision and clarity, the relatively neglected possibility of what I identified as "impartially benevolent free riding," understood as free riding motivated by impartial benevolence. This possibility is related to the fact that even an impartially benevolent agent can favor allowing for some free rides, wherein an action that will be burdensome for an agent is omitted with only a trivial cost to the whole. The problem raised by impartially benevolent free riding is that, insofar as there is nothing distinctive about the instance in question, the sort of benevolent thinking under consideration can, when generalized over individuals or over time, result in an important shared goal never being met. Overall, the discussion in Section 1 revealed reasons for thinking that, without restraint, certain benefits of cooperation and self-control may be out of reach.

Section 2 reviewed various precommitment strategies and related positions regarding them. Such strategies, which can involve mutual coercion mutually agreed upon or self-control via self-constraint, can sometimes be used to straightforwardly solve Prisoner's Dilemma situations that threaten to rob agents of the potential benefits of cooperation or self-control. Precommitment devices can, however, be costly and are not always readily available. As such, addressing cooperative dilemmas and self-control problems is not always a simple matter. This was illustrated via a review of the predicament of the persistent procrastinator who, though genuinely and seriously concerned about her failure to make progress on a proclaimed priority, is subject to second-order procrastination because identifying and settling on a simple solution to her procrastination problem is itself a challenge. Section 2 closed with a discussion of Ulysses contracts – a precommitment device that, though particularly controversial, can, in some cases, also be dilemma-resolving in a way that gives the constrained self a stake in having the contract accepted as legitimately enforceable.

Section 3 considered the possibility of rational resoluteness, wherein rational agents can reliably resolve to adhere to a cooperative or self-controlled course of action (or set of actions) and follow through without having to introduce the sorts of constraints involved in the precommitment devices considered in

Section 2. I reviewed prominent defenses of rational resoluteness, considered existing challenges to these defenses, and articulated some new challenges. Along the way, I developed some new ideas and arguments concerning resoluteness and quasi-resoluteness via an appeal to the importance of meta-considerations and a careful examination of cases of temptation in which there is a risk of the sort of impartially benevolent free riding introduced in Section 1. In such cases, being quasi-resolute may be more advantageous than being strictly resolute.

Section 4 focused on condensing and synthesizing some results that show that much of the current debate on commitment and resoluteness in rational action abstracts away from some very important complications concerning the nature of actions and the nature of intentions. After explaining the relevant complications, I explained how they impact some of the discussions earlier in the Element. In particular, I revisited my earlier discussion of impartially benevolent free riding and suggested that, despite initial appearances to the contrary in the sorts of cases of failure involving free riding motivated by impartial benevolence that I consider, *not* all of the doings (or omissions) occurring at points on the way to failure in relation to the goal at stake are at most trivially detrimental relative to the goal. I also revisited the apparent contrast between evaluating actions directly and evaluating deliberative procedures, which was featured in a prominent defense of rational resoluteness discussed in Section 3, and suggested that the contrast may be oversimplified, since one cannot be acting intentionally without integrating certain constraints into one's deliberative framework. I then highlighted an alternative contrast, namely the contrast between "on-the-whole" evaluations and evaluations "through time." The aim of Section 4 was to raise some important but understudied questions and to leave the reader with a sufficiently nuanced understanding of the issues.

In the end, it is, I hope, clear that debate regarding the rationality of commitment is connected to some of the most central philosophical debates in ethics, rational choice theory, and action theory, including, for example, debates concerning the connection between rationality and morality, debates concerning the possibility of rational dilemmas, and debates regarding the nature of intentions, actions, and agency. Advances with respect to the first debate are thus important in relation to the latter debates as well.

References

Ainslie, G. (2001). *Breakdown of Will*. Cambridge: Cambridge University Press.

Andreou, C. (2006a). Environmental damage and the puzzle of the self-torturer. *Philosophy & Public Affairs*, **34**(1), 95–108.

(2006b). Might intentions be the only source of practical imperatives. *Ethical Theory and Moral Practice*, **9**(3), 311–325.

(2007a). Environmental preservation and second-order procrastination. *Philosophy & Public Affairs*, **35**(3), 233–248.

(2007b). Understanding procrastination. *Journal for the Theory of Social Behaviour*, **37**(2), 183–193.

(2008). Making a clean break: Addiction and Ulysses contracts. *Bioethics*, **22**(1), 25–31.

(2009). Taking on intentions. *Ratio*, **22**(2), 157–169.

(2010). Coping with procrastination. In *The Thief of Time*, ed. C. Andreou and M. D. White. New York: Oxford University Press, pp. 206–215.

(2014a). The good, the bad, and the trivial. *Philosophical Studies*, **169**(2), 209–225.

(2014b). Temptation, resolutions, and regret. *Inquiry*, **57**(3), 275–292.

(2016). Figuring out how to proceed with evaluation after figuring out what matters. *Dialogue: Canadian Philosophical Review*, **55**, 621–637.

(2018a). Self-paternalism. In *The Routledge Handbook of the Philosophy of Paternalism*, eds. K. Grill and J. Hanna. New York: Routledge, pp. 59–65.

(2018b). Newcomb's problem, rationality, and restraint. In *Newcomb's Problem*, ed. A. Ahmed. Cambridge: Cambridge University Press, pp. 167–178.

(2021). General assessments and attractive exceptions. *Inquiry*, **64**(9), 892–900.

Anscombe, G. E. M. (1963). *Intention*. Cambridge, MA: Harvard University Press.

Bratman, M. (1987). *Intention, Plans, and Practical Reason*. Cambridge, MA: Harvard University Press.

(2018). *Planning, Time, and Self-Governance*. New York: Oxford University Press.

Broome, J. (2001). Are intentions reasons? And how should we cope with incommensurable values? In *Practical Rationality and Preference*, eds. C. W. Morris and A. Ripstein. Cambridge: Cambridge University Press, pp. 98–120.

Davidson, D. (2001). *Essays on Actions and Events*. Oxford: Clarendon Press.

Davidson, D., McKinsey, J. C. C., and Suppes, P. (1955). Outlines of a formal theory of value, I. *Philosophy of Science*, **22**(2), 140–160.

De Condorcet, N. (1785). *Essay on the Application of Analysis to the Probability of Majority Decisions*. Paris, De l'Imprimerie Royale.

Dresser, R. S. (1982). Ulysses and the psychiatrists. *Harvard Civil Rights-Civil Liberties Law Review*, **16**(3), 777–854.

(1984). Bound to treatment. *Hastings Center Report*, **14**(3), 13–16.

Elster, J. (1984). *Ulysses and the Sirens: Studies in Rationality and Irrationality*. Cambridge: Cambridge University Press.

(2000). *Ulysses Unbound*. Cambridge: Cambridge University Press.

Ferrero, L. (2017). Intending, acting, and doing. *Philosophical Explorations*, **20**(S2), S13–S39.

Gauthier, D. (1986). *Morals by Agreement*. Oxford: Clarendon Press.

(1991). Why contractarianism? In *Contractarianism and Rational Choice*, ed. P. Vallentyne. Cambridge: Cambridge University Press, pp. 15–30.

(1994). Assure and threaten. *Ethics*, **104**(4), 690–721.

Glover, J. (1975). It makes no difference whether or not I do it (I). *Proceedings of the Aristotelian Society*, Supplementary Volumes, **49**(1), 171–190.

Gollwitzer, P. M. and Schaal, B. (1998). Metacognition in action: The importance of implementation intentions. *Personality and Social Psychology Review*, **2**(2), 124–136.

Hansson, S. O. and Grüne-Yanoff, T. (2017). Preferences. In *Stanford Encyclopedia of Philosophy*, ed. E. N. Zalta. https://plato.stanford.edu/entries/preferences/

Hardin, G. (1968). The tragedy of the commons. *Science*, **162**(3859), 1243–1248.

Hobbes, T. (1668/1994). *Leviathan*. Indianapolis: Hackett.

Holton, R. (2009). *Willing, Wanting, Waiting*. Oxford: Clarendon Press.

Hume, D. (1951/1998). *An Enquiry Concerning the Principles of Morals*, ed. T. L. Beauchamp. Oxford: Clarendon Press.

Kagan, S. (2011). Do I make a difference? *Philosophy & Public Affairs*, **39**(2), 105–141.

Kavka, G. (1983). The toxin puzzle. *Analysis*, **43**(1), 33–36.

McClennen, E. (1990). *Rationality and Dynamic Choice*. Cambridge: Cambridge University Press.

(1998). Rationality and rules. In *Modeling Rationality, Morality, and Evolution*, ed. P. Danielson. New York: Oxford University Press, pp. 13–40.

Olson, M., Jr. (1965). *The Logic of Collective Action*. Cambridge, MA: Harvard University Press.

Parfit, D. (1984). *Reasons and Persons*. Oxford: Oxford University Press.

Peterson, M. (2015). *The Prisoner's Dilemma*. Cambridge: Cambridge University Press.

Quante, M. (1999). Precedent autonomy and personal identity. *Kennedy Institute of Ethics Journal*, **9**(4), 365–381.

Quinn, W. (1993). The puzzle of the self-torturer. In *Morality and Action*, ed. Philippa Foot. Cambridge: Cambridge University Press, pp. 198–209.

Rawls, J. (1971). *A Theory of Justice*. Cambridge, MA: Harvard University Press.

Savulescu, J. and Dickenson, D. (1998). The time frame of preferences, dispositions, and the validity of advance directives for the mentally ill. *Philosophy, Psychiatry, and Psychology*, **5**(3), 225–246.

Schelling, T. C. (1984). Ethics, law, and the exercise of self-command. In *Choice and Consequence*. London: Harvard University Press, pp. 83–112.

Spellecy, R. (2003). Reviving Ulysses contracts. *Kennedy Institute of Ethics Journal*, **13**(4), 373–392.

Steele, K. and Stefánsson, H. O. (2020). Decision theory. In *Stanford Encyclopedia of Philosophy*, ed. E. N. Zalta. https://plato.stanford.edu/archives/win2020/entries/decision-theory/

Temkin, L. S. (2012). *Rethinking the Good*. Oxford: Oxford University Press.

Tenenbaum, S. (2020). *Rational Powers in Action*. New York: Oxford University Press.

Tenenbaum, S. and Raffman, D. (2012). Vague projects and the puzzle of the self-torturer. *Ethics*, **123**(1), 86–112.

Thoma, J. (2018). Temptation and preference-based instrumental rationality. In *Self-Control, Rationality, and Decision Theory*, ed. J. L. Bermúdez. Cambridge: Cambridge University Press, pp. 27–47.

Thompson, M. (2008). *Life and Action*. Cambridge, MA: Harvard University Press.

Vanderschraaf, P. (2006). The circumstances of justice. *Politics, Philosophy & Economics*, **5**(3), 321–351.

Velleman, J. D. (2000). Deciding how to decide. In *The Possibility of Practical Reason*. Oxford: Oxford University Press, pp. 221–243.

Acknowledgments

My thanks to Martin Peterson and Hilary Gaskin for their feedback on my plan for this Element and for giving me the opportunity to both survey some intriguing terrain and rework, synthesize, and add to some of my prior contributions in the space. Thanks also to participants at the 2021 *Workshop on Desire and Motivation* for stimulating discussion and to two anonymous reviewers for their helpful comments on the penultimate draft of this Element. I am grateful for supporting research funds from the University of Utah and from the Charles H. Monson Esteemed Faculty Award. The Whiteley Center provided a much appreciated peaceful and inspirational setting for some of the writing of this Element.

Cambridge Elements ☰

Decision Theory and Philosophy

Martin Peterson
Texas A&M University

Martin Peterson is Professor of Philosophy and Sue and Harry E. Bovay Professor of the History and Ethics of Professional Engineering at Texas A&M University. He is the author of four books and one edited collection, as well as many articles on decision theory,ethics and philosophy of science.

About the Series

This Cambridge Elements series offers an extensive overview of decision theory in its many and varied forms. Distinguished authors provide an up-to-date summary of the results of current research in their fields and give their own take on what they believe are the most significant debates influencing research, drawing original conclusions.

Cambridge Elements ≡

Decision Theory and Philosophy

Elements in the Series

Printed in the United States
by Baker & Taylor Publisher Services